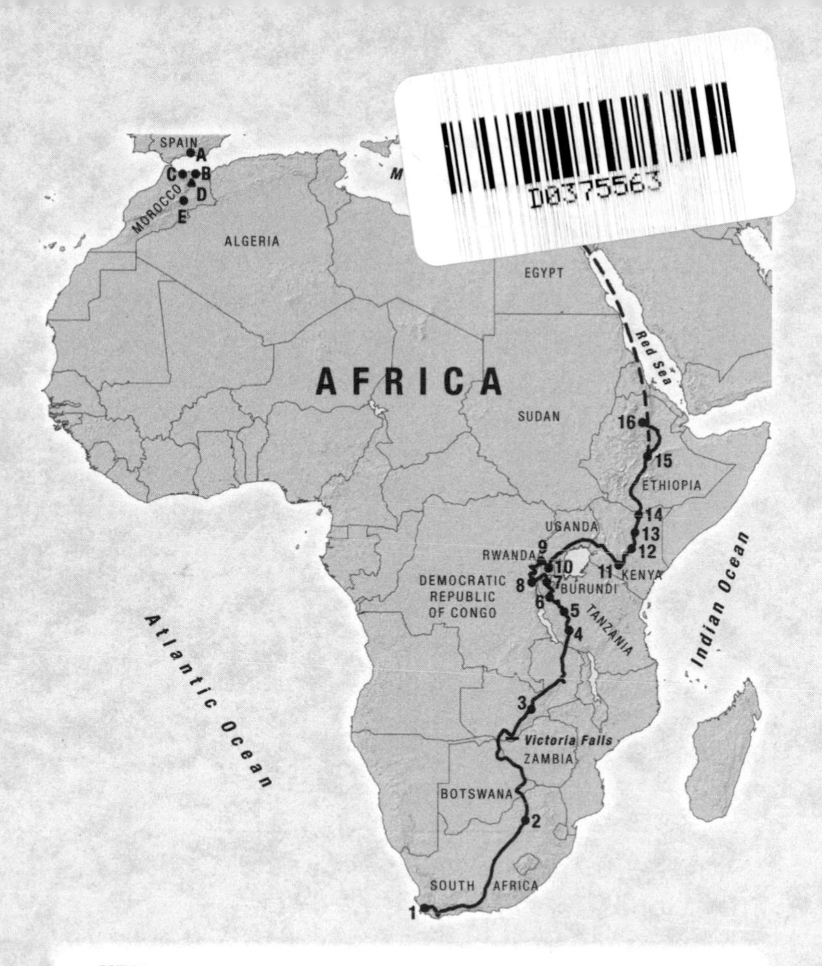

D0375563

KEY:

A Malaga
B Melilla
C Al Hoceima
D Mount Gurugu
E Fez
1 Cape Town
2 Johannesburg
3 Lusaka
4 Sumbawanga
5 Mpanda
6 Kigoma
7 Bujumbura
8 Bukavu
9 Goma
10 Kigali
11 Nairobi
12 Isiolo
13 Marsabit
14 Moyale
15 Addis Ababa
16 Lalibela
17 Cairo

The Only Road North

9,000 Miles of Dirt and Dreams

ERIK MIRANDETTE

ZONDERVAN.com/
AUTHORTRACKER
follow your favorite authors

The Only Road North
Copyright © 2007 by Erik Mirandette

Requests for information should be addressed to:

Zondervan, *Grand Rapids, Michigan 49530*

Library of Congress Cataloging-in-Publication Data

Mirandette, Erik, 1983-
The only road north : 9,000 miles of dirt and dreams / Erik Mirandette.
p. cm.
ISBN-13: 978-0-310-27435-3
ISBN-10: 0-310-27435-4
1. Africa — Description and travel. 2. Mirandette, Erik, 1983-
— Travel — Africa. 3. Mirandette, Erik, 1983- — Friends and associates.
4. Americans — Travel — Africa. 5. Mirandette, Erik, 1983- — Philosophy.
6. Christian biography. 7. Victims of terrorism — Biography.
8. Terrorism — Egypt — Cairo. I. Title.
DT12.25.M57 2007
916.04'33092 — dc22 [B]

2006033484

Due to the sensitive political situation in some of the countries mentioned, certain names and places have been changed to protect their identities.

All rights reserved. No part of this publication may be reproduced, stored in a retrieval system, or transmitted in any form or by any means — electronic, mechanical, photocopy, recording, or any other — except for brief quotations in printed reviews, without the prior permission of the publisher.

Interior design by Beth Shagene

Printed in the United States of America

07 08 09 10 11 12 13 • 20 19 18 17 16 15 14 13 12 11 10 9 8 7 6 5 4 3

Contents

INTRODUCTION

Kauai, Hawaii

I sit lost on an island somewhere in the Pacific, the rain pattering on the tin roof overhead, the surf crashing in the distance. Here no one knows my name. No one recognizes my face from evening news flashes; no one has heard the stories that haunt me. I came to this island searching for peace. I thought that stepping out of the trivial rush that fills our lives would allow me the time and space to "get better," whatever that means. I am slowly realizing, however, that I will never be "better" as those ignorant to my plight understand the notion. There is no escaping my story. Everywhere I go it burns inside. I can't suppress it any longer. It needs to be told. My only hope is to get it out before it consumes my every thought and emotion.

My story is not what the newspapers made it out to be. It is much bigger than a ten-minute slot on the evening news, something reported with little thought or concern and just as quickly forgotten. My story is bigger than me. It is bigger than any one of us. My story is of our wildest dreams coming true and our most godless fears and horrors being realized. It is of love and hate, life and death, brotherhood and utter solitude, faith and doubt.

The last thing this world needs is another self-help or feel-good-faith book, seven simple steps to whatever. Just the thought makes my stomach turn. The truth is that life is far too complex to be put in a box, labeled, and have the appropriate manual attached. I wonder, have those people who seem to have all the answers ever really experienced hardship or grief, true joy, or adventure? Have they ever really lived? For those of us who venture outside the cookie-cutter lives that many settle for, a superficial, plastic faith with the corresponding instruction booklet will do nothing. When we take that brave step from the comfortable mainstream into the unknown, we quickly discover that we are all just travelers on a journey trying to find our way.

I write to you as a mere seeker, a fellow traveler on the road that is life, a believer in truth, trusting in hope. I have scoured books, stared endlessly into the night sky, and cried out to the heavens searching for answers. There are none to be had. And yet there remains an ever so faint whisper coming from within. It is all I have left. It is my compass; it is my guide.

My story offers no resolution and has no ending. It is not nice or neat, but it is real. I have given up trying to make sense of it; rather I will tell it as only I can, as I experienced it. I invite you to share my experiences, to join me on this journey, but warn that after a long and trepidant road we will finally arrive before we started, with more questions than answers, completely and totally unsettled, but ever searching, ever hopeful.

This is my story ...

ERIK MIRANDETTE
March 2006

WHISPERS THE VOICE WITHIN

Colorado Springs, Colorado

A time comes in everyone's life when purpose calls. We each have a unique legend to live, and that legend seeks us out, hoping desperately that we will notice it—and embrace it.

I was nineteen years old when I first felt it whisper.

A sophomore at the Air Force Academy, I had convinced myself that I was doing everything right, that I was taking the road less traveled. I had gone to the academy fresh out of high school, a boy full of ideals, determined to help save the world. It would be an arduous four years, but I believed that a service academy would best equip me to make a difference in this world—and for me that was worth the hardship.

By superficial standards I was doing well: I had made the dean's list despite a challenging major; I was a pole-vaulter on the track and field team; I even helped on the student council. But as good as I may have looked from the outside, I was a mess inside—unhappy, overstressed, and restless. I knew that I was not living the life I was meant to live.

At first I dismissed the feeling. I mean, sure, I was drinking a lot, and things were always up and down with my girlfriend—but this was the standard melodrama of college life. I was a college student doing what I thought college students did. Besides, everyone gets anxious from time to time when stuck in the daily grind. Life was busy and I was tired. Of course I wasn't content. Life at that time was something to be endured, not enjoyed. I would start really living after I graduated. That's when I'd see the world. That's when I'd make my difference. The meantime was just something I had to get through.

But as the months dragged on I realized that my ideals, my reasons for joining the academy, were no longer what fueled me. They were quickly fading and cynicism was filling the void. I dreaded my classes. I loathed my studies. I had forgotten almost entirely why I was subjecting myself to such a strenuous credit load at such a rigid university. In time, my reason to continue wasn't the pursuit of some righteous cause as it had once been. If I had a reason at all anymore, aside from habit, it was to get through the week so I could have sex with my girlfriend on Friday and party on Saturday. I tried to make church on Sunday—and then inevitably ended up still hung over in class the following Monday, counting the hours until the weekend. This had become my routine.

I broke up with my girlfriend and quit drinking myself into a stupor every weekend. Surprisingly, after taking those steps toward self-improvement, after appeasing my conscience and kicking my vices, I didn't feel any less unsettled. If anything, the restlessness grew.

I was going to jump out of my skin if I didn't change something. I needed to quiet this voice inside me.

Something had to happen.

Early one frosty Colorado morning I was jammed into the back of a buddy's car on my way to the airport for two precious weeks off—Christmas break. In the front seat I heard Rob, an upperclassman who lived next door to me, chatting with another passenger about two years he recently had spent in Russia serving as a missionary. Two years in a faraway land? The adventurer in me needed to know more. How was it possible to just leave for two years and come back to resume your studies?

I hadn't known much about Rob before that morning. His room was right next to mine, but he sort of kept to himself. I had never sensed any arrogance about him. He was always kind in passing. Physically he was not exceptional, but his demeanor spoke of unshakable character and confidence. He seemed to exist and operate on a totally different level than most guys I knew. One could tell just by looking at him that he was above the boyish ignorance that consumed my friends—and my nights. He had an air about him that demanded respect.

Now I understood. He had seen the world; he knew of foreign lands and spoke a strange language. He had something that set him apart, something that was impossible to learn, something that could be forged only in the fires of experience. I knew then what I had to do.

I went home to Michigan and spent the holidays with my brother and my parents. I told them all about my new plan. I would leave my teammates, my friends, and my classes at the academy and move somewhere in the world to help people for two years. The specifics were yet unplanned, but the idea was solid in my mind.

I could do little that actually surprised my family—they were accustomed to my jump-with-both-feet approach to life—but upon hearing my plan they did manage to raise a couple of points worth consideration. I had survived basic training and the hazing of freshman year. I had invested grueling effort into my studies and was only two and a half years away from graduation. If I were to leave, readmittance would not be guaranteed. I would risk forfeiting my education and commission—and all over a thought that wasn't even a day old. My plan, as noble as it sounded to me, was in reality unpractical, improbable, and most likely financially impossible.

+

Five months later, after a dozen emails and two phone calls, I found myself on a plane destined for north Africa. I was nervous, but it didn't matter. I had taken that step. I had listened to the voice within.

In my wildest dreams I couldn't have conjured up more fantastic adventures than those that awaited me. I would have never thought that I would journey through the Sahara on camels or that I would run with the bulls in Pamplona.

I certainly didn't know that I would encounter a reclusive young Muslim man named Hassan and the seductive ideology of a fanatical imam urging him to make the ultimate sacrifice in the name of God.

If I had known the results of the horrors that lay ahead, would I have shut my ears to the voice inside me urging me on? Would I have given up the life I was meant to live to spare the pain that was to come?

My Cameroonian friends and I.

Hit the Ground Running

Melilla, Spain

The awkward little twin-prop plane looked like something you would see filled with clowns at a circus. I never would have thought it capable of flight if I wasn't sitting five thousand feet over the Mediterranean headed south. I repositioned myself in my seat and swallowed hard. My throat was killing me. I hoped it was just the dry June air, but I knew better. That cute little blonde waitress that I took out for dinner on one of my last nights in the States had said something about a sore throat.

All around me sat Arab women covered from head to toe in what looked like bedsheets. Beside them sat men with big beards in *jalabas*, an unattractive garment unique to the Arab world. I was wearing a T-shirt and shorts and was uncomfortably hot. My fellow travelers must have been roasting under all of those clothes.

The engines droned on. I checked my watch again. The flight had left an hour late from Spain and we had already been airborne ten minutes longer than scheduled. We should have landed by now. The pilot came over the intercom and announced something in Spanish. The other passengers looked uneasy. Everyone fastened seatbelts. The plane banked and out my window I got my first view of the African coast. Below me lay the small city of Melilla — my destination.

A few months earlier my church back home had put me in touch with a humanitarian worker they support who said he could use some extra help. For the last twenty years Paul had been based with his family in this Spanish town nestled on the northern coast of Africa. He was involved in countless developmental humanitarian projects and headed up a group called Partnerships International. Those who knew him spoke his name with reverence as one might a distinguished war hero. I had spoken with him on the phone only twice, but after telling him a little about myself and what I was hoping to do — i.e., help thy fellow man for a couple years — he encouraged me to raise some support and get a plane ticket. He had much to do and one could always use another pair of hands in his line of business. So that's what I did. I didn't really know what I would be doing to help out — or even many specifics about Partnerships International. All that I knew was that there was a place for me in his organization.

I gazed out my window and watched Melilla grow from just an idea in the distance to a living, breathing city full of flesh-and-blood people. The knot in my stomach pulled tighter. I thought about my younger brother, Alex, about my mom and dad. I felt like I did the first time I moved away from home. I was nervous, but confident that I would be able to handle whatever awaited me. I was ready to do something for someone other than myself.

The plane landed hard; we skipped once ... twice ... three times before we were finally on the ground. We taxied to our gate — if that's what this slab of weathered concrete was called — and filed off the aircraft. Hot, humid air smacked me in the face.

Inside the airport I looked around — the only blond-haired, blue-eyed kid in north Africa searching for another American face. The other passengers had either been met by their families or walked out to their cars. For a moment I stood alone.

Then a smiling man with kind eyes greeted me with a familiar accent. "Erik Mirandette, I presume."

"The one and only," I responded in a cocky tone.

"I'm Paul. Welcome to Melilla. Are you hungry?"

"Starving."

✦

It didn't take long to find my niche on the Melilla team. Paul had plenty of errands for me: on any given week I would run medical supplies to some clinic in Morocco or visit with partners in some remote village. I had picked up a functional level of Arabic quickly and handled myself well representing our humanitarian organization, or NGO as they are often referred to. Whenever an odd job needed done, I was the one they would call. I was becoming the go-to boy.

My job was interesting and my role was important. However, I had too much free time. I normally spent two or three days every week traveling and actually working, but that left four or five days totally open. I needed more.

One unseasonably chilly fall morning, I went for a run through the center shopping area of Melilla. The usual west African refugees were guarding cars in the street, letting their owners go about their business certain that no one would vandalize or rob their vehicles while they were away. The refugees huddled together trying to conserve each others' body heat while they waited for the sun to get high enough to shine directly down on them from between the buildings. The shops had just opened and cars were filling the parking spots. A woman came out of an overpriced shoe store with a new pair of knee-high, white and pink, rhinestone-laden boots that she would probably wear twice before they found their way to the trash. One of the refugees who was guarding that spot jumped up to stop traffic and help her back out. This guy wasn't wearing shoes. He had two winter jackets but no shirt underneath. His pants had holes, which clearly revealed that he didn't have underwear. He was wearing two pairs of socks, holes worn through both, and was obviously very cold. I saw him look longingly at the lady's bag. His eyes screamed, yet he smiled and said nothing. The lady drove off without giving him a cent; she didn't even acknowledge his existence. The refugee silently rejoined the group standing on the corner.

I couldn't blame the woman for buying an expensive pair of boots. I mean, I wear a $120 pair of Doc Martens. What struck me was the reason she didn't give the refugee so much as a small coin after spending €150 (about $190) on such a frivolous item for herself: if she had acknowledged his presence, she would have felt guilty for buying her boots. She did what everyone did in Melilla, something that I had not specifically noticed until that moment: she ignored the need altogether.

That scene stuck with me for several days. After I noticed it once, I began to see it happen everywhere every day. I asked Paul about the refugees—where did they come from and how did they survive? What could be done to help them? But the darkest and most dangerous of tribulations are always greater than they first appear—and the refugees' situation, I would soon learn, was no different.

A week passed just like the weeks before. I climbed down the cliffs that surrounded the sea to the hidden beach that was not far from my house, I studied the Spanish language every afternoon, I made a couple quick day trips into Morocco to deliver supplies — but once again the restlessness inside had been awakened. The voice began to whisper.

I thought of the refugees constantly, both those in Melilla and those who were no doubt worse off on the other side of the merciless Spanish border. When I ate, I wondered what they were eating. When I lay in my bed at night covered by my comfortable blanket, I wondered what shelter separated them from the frosty evenings.

Then Paul approached me and said that he was going to take three doctors visiting from America into Morocco for a day to share the needs of the region. Though it hadn't originally been a planned stop, he told me they were going to swing by the dump on Mount Gurugu, just south of Melilla, where most of the refugees hoping to get through Spain's heavily guarded border lived. I was welcome to come along, but he emphasized that we would just be passing through; no one was to get out of the van. I was thrilled. Finally an opportunity to see the faces of the men I had been thinking so much about — and, if I was lucky, to start developing a plan to provide them aid.

That afternoon we navigated the chaotic border, stopping at a bakery on the way to pick up a hundred fresh loaves of bread for a whopping sum of 100 dirham (about $10). The road snaked up Gurugu toward the black plume of smoke that marked the trash dump. As we approached, I began to distinguish figures in the distance. The closer we got, the more I noticed shadows hidden behind boulders and bushes cautiously following our car with uneasy eyes. Finally we reached the last cutback before the dump.

As the car turned the corner, a scene was revealed that is to this very day seared into my mind. Before me stood the silhouettes of hundreds of men only partially visible through the smoke. They were crouched over, wading through the burning sea of refuse, sifting through the filth in search of some edible morsel. This was their only source of food. Dozens of men—covered with rashes, cuts, and boils—came running up to the sides of the van. Some of their stomachs were protruding abnormally from under their tattered shirts, a sure sign that parasites lived within. The stench of the burning trash descended upon us passengers in the van all at once, sucking the breath from our lungs. I can still taste the choking smoke. I found myself feeling physically sick.

At least fifty sickly black faces pressed against the car windows, all eyeing the loaves of bread. Paul shouted to me over the longing cries of the refugees to hand him the bread. He sped up the van, putting some distance between us and the crowd, then opened the door and gave all of the bread to a smaller group of hungry men. The crowd sprinted to the bread, thanking us profusely. They all took as much as they could stand to eat and stuffed it into their mouths, as does a dog that doesn't know when it will be fed again. The truth was that their stomachs were the only safe place to keep the little food they had been given. As we continued up the mountain toward a little known pass, I stared from the back of the van at the mass of human beings reduced to jackals.

We had spent no more than five minutes in the dump with the refugees, but the scene had made a tremendous impression on all of us. The group didn't say much as Paul showed us the other needs of the region. I understood why the refugees were not originally a planned part of the tour. It was difficult to take anything else that day very seriously after what we had just witnessed.

My bedroom window in Melilla faced directly south from the hilltop and looked right onto Mount Gurugu. I could see the black smoke curl into the sky. If I looked hard enough my mind started to see men with a heart and soul just like mine, diseased and dying as they crawled through the refuse. I found myself staring out the window watching the day fade. Then the single light on the mountain that marked the dump carried me into the night. Every moment I was in my room the mountain hung surreally out my window. The voice that I had followed across the world in search of my purpose was calling loud and clear.

✦

Over the next few days I researched why we weren't doing anything to help these men. We were a government-recognized humanitarian organization. Why didn't we have some sort of relief effort in place? Surely something could be done. I found my answer, but it wasn't what I was expecting.

These refugees leave their homes in central and west Africa for any number of reasons. Many of their countries have been consumed by war, their families have been killed or relocated, and for them home is nothing more than a figment of the past. Some live in desperate poverty and have heard about the unimaginable wealth in Europe and the United States. They leave their homes in pursuit of a better life. Some are just kids dreaming of adventure, discontent with their circumstances.

Of the thousands of refugees who depart sub-Saharan Africa every year, the majority struggle toward Spain—the geographically closest and thus most attainable country in Europe. Five thousand kilometers of merciless desert, corrupt border officials, and the virtually impenetrable Spanish border, backed by lethal force, are just some of the obstacles that separate them from a new world. Most of these difficulties they will have to face on foot with no resources. The desert claims many; the border stops the rest. Those few who somehow manage to make it into Spain are free to travel anywhere in the European Union. They risk it all for that slim chance.

Millions around the world would kill to have my passport and the citizenship it signifies; every day hundreds die trying. However, this sad truth does not enable America and Europe to open their borders and welcome one and all. Our borders would be quickly overrun and the situation here would be no better than the situation that the refugees are trying to escape. Europe is already saturated with African refugees, and Spain has become known as the door through which the majority passes. As a result the European Union has put increasing pressure on the Spanish government to end this incessant flow of immigration. Spain has in turn put pressure on the Moroccan government, whose methods are less scrutinized, to rid their borders of these pestering refugees.

Offering any type of aid or assistance to refugees is a punishable offense in Morocco. Any humanitarian organization that hopes to continue to work in Morocco has to pick its battles and leave that situation alone. The hundreds of men that I had seen earlier at Gurugu were caught in the balance of a deadly political game.

The problem was too sensitive for an NGO to become involved. Something more low-profile needed to be done, something less conspicuous. I could plainly see that the refugees' situation weighed heavily on Paul's heart, but years of exposure to this sort of desperation had instilled in him a cold discernment absolutely essential to the character of any humanitarian. I asked if he would be opposed to my making weekly trips to the refugees to bring them bread and medicine. It would be a personal project, done on my own time in addition to my current responsibilities, totally unaffiliated with Partnerships International. He seemed to be both nervous and relieved, and reluctantly gave me the go-ahead.

I started plotting immediately. The following Saturday I borrowed a car and left just as the sun was beginning to rise. I crossed into Morocco, filled the car with bread, and drove up the road toward the black smoke.

Only a dozen men were in the dump when I arrived. Most people in Melilla were still sleeping; I had hoped the case would be the same with the refugees. I had more than enough bread for everyone and plenty to be taken back to their friends. I parked the car further up the road and handed out the food. It was much more relaxed and controlled than the last time I went. I used the opportunity to talk with the refugees. I asked them their names, where they lived. What were their biggest problems, their greatest needs? I told them my name and that I would be back the following week at the same time with more bread. Two men, Mustafa and Emanuel, invited me back to their camp so I could speak with their community leader. I was shocked. "You mean to tell me that you all live in community somewhere in these forests and that there are leaders among you?"

I followed my guides a couple of miles away from the road down a steep trail through dense forest. We crossed over a stream and then up a different trail to the top of another ridge. This was where they lived. There were hundreds of rudimentary shelters built from wood found in the forest and whatever scraps of plastic or cardboard they were able to pull out of the dump. The shelters certainly didn't look sufficient. The men had divided into communities based on their country of origin, and each community had elected a chairman. Mustafa and Emanuel were both from Cameroon and spoke good English. They led me to their community. It was relatively small with only thirty-five members, located at the periphery of the camp.

I knew right away that this was the perfect place to start. I would be able to come and go without drawing too much unnecessary attention to myself, but still begin to build trust with the refugees. I waited as my two guides went to get the community chairman. Their robust leader came down to meet me wearing a smile and warmly welcomed me into their camp.

At that time about eight hundred men (and apparently a number of women as well, though I rarely saw any) were hiding in the forests of Gurugu, the living testaments to the problems of seven or eight different sub-Saharan countries.

What could possibly have been going on in their countries to make so many of them choose this fate?

The two primary languages spoken among the refugees were English and French. My Cameroonian friends were mostly francophone, but a few spoke English. Their whole community crowded around the chairman and me as he revealed that their biggest problem was not the parasites or the sicknesses or malnutrition or cold; it was the raids. In addition to inhibiting anyone from providing aid, the Moroccan police and military jointly carried out weekly raids on the camps, stealing anything of value and burning the rest. Clothes, food, shelter—nothing was spared. Every week it was all taken or destroyed, and every week it was all rebuilt. As if that were not enough, the Moroccan government would also capture as many of the refugees as they were able to during the raid, beat them, and then drop them off in the middle of the desert between the Moroccan and Algerian border. They were left with the simple instructions to go back to their countries and were offered no food or water for the journey.

A couple of the men stepped forward, showing me healed bullet wounds.

"They try to kill us, man," one announced.

I was overwhelmed. Who could look at these men's faces and not feel compassion? What kind of a monster could inflict harm on someone so terribly desperate? When I asked the chairman what were his community's greatest needs, his tone caught my attention right away. He spoke as a general in the middle of battle might to long-overdue reinforcements. He might as well have asked, "What took you so long?"

He was not trying to elicit pity; he was not even asking me to help. He was simply stating a fact with the full confidence that I would do my best to meet the needs.

"Medicine, food, clothing, and Bibles," he answered. His last word caught me so by surprise that I asked him to repeat it.

"Bibles. They are our greatest need. We have been asking God for help for a long time. It is good that you are here. You are a man of God, are you not?" I froze, and I think my heart skipped a beat. I looked around at the faces of these desperate men. Me, a man of God? I wasn't really sure what I believed until a couple of months ago, and now I was a man of God?

"Umm, yeah," I answered.

"Good, then will you pray for us?"

A pastor from the community stepped forward and bowed his head. I had prayed in a group, I think, once in my life before that day. And here I was now, in front of all these men, completely shocked and confused. I couldn't say no, but I sure didn't feel like it was my place to lead them in prayer. An awkward moment passed before I closed my eyes, lifted my head, and opened my mouth. I thanked God for bringing me there. I asked him to give me the means to help these desperate men on the mountain and though I didn't say it out loud, I also thanked him for showing me where I fit, where my part was in the grand scheme of things. Any doubt that I ever had about faith, about calling, about my place in the world was gone. I had heeded the whisper's instruction and chased the notion that I was created to fulfill a specific purpose of the utmost importance more than four thousand miles, over an ocean and across three continents. As I stood there in the center of that group, I knew that I had found the treasure I sought.

I still had responsibilities as part of the Melilla team. I traveled through Morocco delivering supplies to groups and visiting partners, but the refugees occupied my every thought. Right after my trip to Gurugu, I had to spend a few days in Morocco, but the next Saturday was fast approaching and I had given my word. I began to ask at local pharmacies for expired medicine. I sent updates out to all of my contributors, explaining the situation on Gurugu and asking for donations specifically for the refugees. I scrounged around all of the team's houses to get any English Bibles they could spare. I was unable to get a car that wasn't affiliated with Partnerships International, so my next trip to Gurugu would have to be on foot. All of the antiparasitics, antibiotics, anti-inflammatories, and Bibles that I was able to muster up could easily fit inside one backpack. It was not the load I had hoped to deliver, but just my consistent presence was worth the trip.

I crossed the border early and headed toward the black smoke. An hour or two later I found my friend Mustafa, who took me through the different communities, distributing what we thought the most appropriate medicine to those who needed it. I reserved the Bibles for the pastors of the communities. Several communities asked "Mr. Erik, a man of God" to pray for them, as if I were at all worthy of such a title. I took some photos. The landscape of the camps had changed drastically in the past week. Apparently the Moroccan authorities had carried out an assault just four days earlier. I gave many of the men my email address and phone number in case they ever made it to Melilla. I tried to encourage those I could and promised I would be back.

This trip was not inconspicuous; everyone had heard about the American with food and medicine. All eyes were on me—some were welcoming and hopeful, others were skeptical and questioning. I was escorted to the camp of those who were injured and couldn't walk without a cane. These men had no hope of ever getting out of Gurugu, but surviving elsewhere was even harder ... so they sat and waited and asked God for a miracle. I took some more photos and prayed with them. Prayer was becoming the thing that I did when I knew I could do nothing else. The men always asked for it, and it let me feel like I had done more than just gawk at their misery. I spent the whole day in the camps, talking with different people, meeting leaders, and taking pictures. I ran out of my medicine early and the Bibles went just as quickly, but the men knew I would be back with more.

The last of the communities was the Nigerian ghetto. This was the largest in the camp, numbering about one hundred and fifty. The sun was getting low and I would soon lose the light altogether. The whole community gathered around as I spoke with the leader who very passionately voiced the struggles and sufferings of his people. Finally a man approached who was gravely ill. One could tell just by looking at him that death was near. "When Ike dies ..." they would say right in front of him.

I looked at his face and I could hear his soul cry. But it was true; he would die just as so many others had before him. He needed medical attention. His friends begged me to smuggle him into Melilla where he might see a doctor. But I couldn't. They begged me to talk to the doctors and bring them to him, but who would I talk to? They wouldn't come. I couldn't stand this being a public conversation any longer and pulled Ike aside. As he fought tears, I tried to record his symptoms as best as I could. Among other things he was coughing blood, his whole body was swollen like a water balloon, and when it got cold he couldn't breathe. The pastor and I prayed for him. Tears built behind his closed eyes. One more time he begged that I take him with me back into Melilla. Would it have been possible? Would I have been able to save this man? It would mean risking everything to smuggle a refugee through the Spanish border, but could I have saved this one? I looked deep into his pleading eyes and said the only thing I could. "I'm sorry."

There were so many.

It was dark and I still had to find my way down the mountain to the car. Ike didn't want to see me leave. I was his last hope. He and I both knew that if I left without him, I would never see him again. Many more came to speak to me, but I had to go. "I will be back next week. I'll bring more medicine and food."

I tripped down the valley until I finally reached the shady border. The Moroccans eyed me suspiciously as I crossed the hundred feet of chaotic no-man's land where smugglers and thieves lurked in plain view and wild dogs roamed, back into the peace and safety of Europe. I got home utterly exhausted—physically, mentally, and emotionally. Part of me was ecstatic—I had found what I had been searching for, there was no doubt about it. But this was no game; this was not the happy feel-good contribution I had expected. Who was I to be the hope for these people? I felt completely inadequate. I had sought purpose, but this was so much more. People were dying and they looked to me as their only help. I began to question if I had taken on more than I was prepared for.

Despite the doubt, I knew that my visiting Gurugu was more than just a self-originating impulse. Something inexplicable had led me there. If I believed that God had brought me to the refugees, then I must also believe that he considered me worthy and capable of the task. Could it be that I was capable of far more than I had ever thought or imagined?

I knew that I would never be able to meet all the needs of the refugees. Men would still die, but that didn't take away from the good that I could do. My efforts could feed a hungry man, they could cure a sick man, and they could encourage a defeated man. No matter what, I had to go back. They were counting on me.

The following night a small group of refugees traveled down the mountain into a nearby city. It was a bold move—to be seen in a city could have meant arrest and deportation, but they had a message for me that couldn't wait until next Saturday.

✦

I checked my email Monday expecting the usual message from my brother or maybe a friend back home. Much to my surprise a message waiting in my inbox was simply signed "Gurugu." It read:

"We know who you is, we all know what you did, a bad brother is what you be. The next time you come to Gurugu we will kill you. Please stay away. Death is waiting for you here. We are all waiting for you to come and die."

As I read the words of the refugees' letter, my heart sank into my stomach. I had no idea what had provoked such a threat. What had happened to make the hopeful faces I had left just two days earlier say this? Who sent it? Was it a single man infuriated by God-knows-what, or did it represent a community—or all of the refugees? Surely Mustafa, Ike, and Emanuel had no part in it. Had the Cameroonian community turned on me?

I wondered if they would really kill me. There was no authority on the mountain; these men were already wanted outlaws just for being in Morocco. If they killed me, no one would be there to question it. Also, these men were not your average twenty-five-year-olds from white suburbia. These men had seen war. Many had witnessed the gruesome deaths of family members. They themselves were dying in that forest. Who among them would have blinked at the death of some white kid they knew nothing about?

Until that point I had never traveled to Gurugu with anything of value aside from the supplies that I was giving away. I never felt in danger because it wouldn't have been to anyone's advantage to harm me. My safety net until that point was that the refugees would benefit most from my leaving because I would come back with more aid. But now my coming back with more aid was the very thing that they had warned me against.

The email did frighten me. This was the first time my life had legitimately been threatened, but more than frightened I felt awful that I had become one more thing on the long list that tormented these already desperate men. I wanted so badly to help them in whatever way I could, but now they thought that I was another enemy seductively trying to harm them. My heart was broken.

I was torn. Could I go back? To do so was to risk death. Could I not? I had found a cause worthy of my life—was it worth risking it to continue? My life was no more valuable than any one of theirs, and if I did continue how many lives could be saved? Even one was enough.

I had already given my life to the pursuit of good. I had been called to fulfill a duty. I believed that God had brought me to Gurugu and I had given my life to the plan I believed he was working all around me. The decision of whether or not I would return to Gurugu had been determined months earlier when I decided that I wanted to realize my part in this plan. They say the coward dies a thousand deaths. I couldn't just give up; I couldn't shy away from this obligation as soon as my own personal comfort and safety had been threatened. To do so would have been to accept certain death. Sure, it would have been more prolonged, but I would for the rest of my days know that I had found my purpose but had been too much of a coward to embrace it. I at least had to learn more.

I knew that I had to return to Gurugu. I knew that I would return. But that didn't ease the tension I felt. I was so afraid.

For the next few days the uneasiness in my stomach grew. I walked through the same streets and went about my business as I had the weeks before. The difference was that next week I may not be here. I tried to eat, but I didn't have much of an appetite. I tried to sleep, but I just lay awake at night wondering, thinking, dreading. The days came and went just as they always do. I called my mom and dad the night before. I called Alex. They noticed I was nervous, but I assured them it was nothing.

"I love you. I'll try to call you again in a few days."

I made the trip on Friday, a day earlier than normal. I stayed in the car until some men I had come to trust approached the vehicle. Emanuel was the first to reach me. He was aware of the threats; the whole camp knew. Apparently a minority was convinced that I worked for the Moroccan government and that I was gathering intel for them. The day after I had visited, another raid occurred in the camps. Several men were injured and a few were shot. Some blamed me for this raid, and the email was their response. But Emanuel assured me that most of the community knew that I was a "man of God," and they begged me to continue making trips to the mountain.

The day went smoothly. I made contact with the refugees and delivered bread without ever stepping out of the car. Now I knew at least one version of the story. To continue making the trips would be to taunt the angry group who wanted me dead, but to abandon the effort altogether would also be to abandon hundreds of people who had been crying out for help and saw the little I could do as their only answer. I couldn't turn my back on them. I had to see this through.

I continued to make my weekly trips to Gurugu. I was more cautious than before but still delivered whatever supplies I could acquire throughout the week. Except for a suspicious minority, the refugees were always thrilled to see me. They would wait alongside the road every Saturday morning and then come running out of the forest as soon as they saw my car approaching. I was becoming very well known on the mountain and in turn I was coming to know its inhabitants not just as refugees but as men with names and stories.

As the weeks passed, I began to exhaust my resources. Everyone I knew who had anything to give to the refugees had already given it, and I was running out of money. The day was fast approaching when I would have nothing left to offer.

It was about this time that a friend of Paul's, a Spaniard named Manolo, approached me. He had heard about my going up the mountain and wanted me to take him too. I was reluctant at first. I wasn't even confident about my own safety there, and if he were to come I would be responsible for both of us. I realized the risk *I* was taking and had come to terms with it, but the thought of risking the life of someone else—a father and a husband—was troubling. This guy has no idea what he is asking to become involved with, I told myself. I didn't speak very good Spanish at that point, and I couldn't adequately explain the gravity of the situation. This job was neither as heroic nor romantic as it may have sounded; it was dirty, it stunk, and I could never do enough. That was the burden that I carried every day, everywhere I went. I put Manolo off for a couple weeks, but he kept on insisting. Finally I gave in.

We departed early Saturday morning as always. The trip went quickly. I met my friends on the mountain, spoke with them, gave them the medicine and food, prayed with them, and then we drove off. We were in Morocco for no more than an hour and Manolo hadn't even gotten out of the car—but the trip had moved him deeply. He didn't say a word the entire ride home. His face wore the same expression as mine the first time I had traveled to Gurugu.

The next day Manolo phoned asking what supplies we needed for the following weekend. It looked like I had a partner. I gave him the standard list—medicine, food, water, and clothes—and told him to bring whatever he could to my house Friday night so we could separate it and load it before the trip on Saturday. He enthusiastically agreed.

That Friday Manolo showed up with a whole carload of supplies—more than I had ever taken to Gurugu in one week. The following Friday the load had almost doubled! He had spoken at his church, sharing his experiences of what was happening just outside the Spanish border, and had implored the people to help.

Together Manolo and I carried donated supplies to the refugees every Saturday. At first we collected all of the donations in my living room. Every Friday night we would sort through the clothes, food, and medicine. Different communities had different needs, and we did our best to meet them. Before long we were receiving so many donations that they wouldn't fit in my house. We moved the collection point to Manolo's church. Over time, organizing the supplies became a churchwide event. All week long they collected supplies and donated money, Friday we would get ready, Saturday we would distribute, and then Sunday Manolo would give the church an update. He had become crucial to the project. I could communicate with the refugees in English, and Manolo could talk in front of the church in Spanish. Together we were a perfect team.

Over the course of the next few months, our weekly trip evolved into a full-out relief effort. Every week we carried hundreds of kilos of food, clothing, and medicine—almost all donated by local Spanish churches. A Spanish nurse volunteered to come along to Gurugu with us for a weekly medical clinic. For three hours the refugees sang worship songs and the pastors spoke while the nurse treated the sick or injured. I would often offer a word of encouragement, always at the refugees' request, and then we would distribute the supplies. Every week the numbers grew. Lives were being saved, faith was being restored, the hungry were being fed, the naked were being clothed. It was a beautiful thing.

As great as the project was and as smooth as it looked from the outside, our trips to the mountain were always very tense. The refugees would whisper in the background about our showing partiality toward one community or another. As much as we were able to bring, it was never enough. More people needed to see the nurse, people needed more medicine than we had to offer. The trips were making a big difference, but at any moment the whole thing could come unglued. And as much time as we spent on that mountain, I knew it was only a matter of time before the Moroccan government would discover us.

Then it happened.

+

It was a beautiful sunshiny day. We got to the mountain early Saturday morning and were met by about one hundred and fifty refugees. Some formed a line to see the nurse; others formed a circle and got ready for the service. Manolo helped the nurse. I greeted the refugees and gave a quick word, then turned the floor over to one of the African pastors. The crowd grew to over three hundred people that day—all singing and clapping. The nurse treated six bullet wounds from raids earlier that week (four others had been shot and killed), one man had severe tuberculosis, and three more were deathly ill with malaria. The rest of the sick and injured had mostly just parasites, bumps, and bruises. Three hours passed and we ran out of medical supplies, much to the disappointment of those in line to see the nurse. The pastors had finished their preaching, and it was time to distribute the food and clothes.

All of the refugees, excited and chattering, gathered on one side of us as we opened the trunks. But then all of a sudden they fell completely silent, not even a whisper among them. I looked up, away from the refugees, to see a single Moroccan policeman emerge from the forest just about one hundred feet behind us. Behind him were no fewer than one hundred Moroccan military and police armed with shotguns and riot gear. This was it. We had been caught in the middle of a raid. One of the pastors stepped forward and yelled to the crowd, "Don't run. Stand together; we are strong together." They all held fast, ready for a war.

The Moroccans were shocked by how many refugees stood before them. They had come expecting to chase individuals through the forest and instead were met by hundreds. The chief of the police got on his radio and shouted in nervous Arabic what I recognized as a call for reinforcements. About two hundred feet separated the refugees and the Moroccans. The Moroccans had the barrels of their guns trained on the wall of refugees, but no one moved. I yelled in English not to do anything—that we would talk to the police.

Manolo and I approached the Moroccans slowly. Their guns stayed on the refugees. Manolo spoke in Spanish to the chief and explained that we had seen these men in need of medical attention so we had treated them and nothing more. He then asked what they were doing with their guns. The chief explained that these men were all illegal immigrants, that he and his comrades had come prepared to arrest and deport twenty of them. If they went peacefully no one would be shot or even beaten. Manolo looked at me. Could we trust this man? If the refugees ran, clubs would drop and bullets would fly. Anarchy. If the Moroccans stayed until reinforcements arrived, they might overrun the entire group. I couldn't speak to Manolo in a language that the Moroccans didn't understand and I didn't want to let them know how much Arabic or Spanish I understood.

I carried the message back to the refugees. Immediately there was confusion. One man shouted, "It's a trick! They will capture us and kill us all!" Another wanted to stay and fight. Most just started to fade into the forest.

One of the pastors looked at me and said, "You tell them that if they swear they will not harm us, twenty of us will go peacefully." He didn't say how they would determine which twenty of them would be arrested. As more of the refugees attempted to sneak off, I shared this word with Manolo, who was still talking with the Moroccan police chief.

I always had a group of African friends that stayed close to me while I was on Gurugu. They helped me organize and carry out the relief every week and watched to make sure that the minority that still wanted me dead kept their distance. This day was no different. They were the last to leave my side. The Moroccans had slowly surrounded the group and started to move in after the crowd had begun to disperse. I was so busy trying to figure out what was going on in this chaotic mix of languages and intentions that I had almost completely lost track of my company.

I'll never forget my dear friend Fidelis. He had stayed by my side through everything and just seconds before the Moroccans grabbed him, he ever so calmly, ever so peacefully, said to me, "Mr. Erik, do you need anything else from me? It is time for me to take care of myself now." I couldn't believe he had stayed. He could have escaped! The only reason he would be taken was because he did not want to leave my side. I looked at the twenty who remained. Fidelis was not the only one. All of my closest friends—all of those guys who helped watch my back and organize the relief—were the ones who had stayed. They would be arrested and deported along with a few of the very sick who were unable to run. For the sick, this arrest was a death sentence.

Just then the reinforcements arrived and went running down into the forest in search of any stragglers that they could arrest. They surrounded us. One Moroccan military member that I will never forget proudly perched himself upon a rock that stood just over us. He pointed the barrel of his shotgun at us. I saw a look in his eyes that I had never seen before that day, a look that I will never forget. He really wanted to kill us. His finger massaged the trigger. He was hoping for the chance to shoot. Looking into his empty eyes sent chills down my spine.

No one died in that exchange, though I never again saw most of those who were arrested. We didn't know if our friends were still alive; we didn't know if they would be released as the Moroccans had agreed. As for Manolo, the nurse, and me, we were arrested and escorted in our cars to the Moroccan police station by a caravan of military and police vehicles. They held us for the day, interrogated us, threatened us, and let us go. Frustrating, yes—but we would be sleeping comfortably in our beds that night.

The car was silent as we slowly drove back toward the Spanish border, the Moroccans following closely behind. Manolo mentioned that we hadn't even had the chance to distribute the food and supplies to the famished refugees. The police had searched our persons and the front of the car, but they never looked in the trunk. We still had a full load of supplies. What were we going to do with it all? Taking things out of Europe wasn't a big deal, but the border guards were much more fussy about what they let in. We would have never gotten through Spanish customs with all of that stuff. We approached the border and our Moroccan escorts, satisfied, continued down the road.

"¿Porque no vamos a Gurugu y dar los alimentos a los refugiados?" I half jokingly suggested. Manolo looked at me, looked up to the light at the dump, and turned the car around. I couldn't believe he was doing it. We were about to end up back in jail, but I was thrilled about the decision. We sped up the road to the base of the dump.

A couple of refugees screamed for joy as soon as they saw our car: "Mr. Erik! Oh, thank God!" We jumped out and unloaded the supplies.

"I don't know when and I don't know how, but we'll be back," I told them. "We're not done. Tell your communities."

Manolo was yelling at me to get into the car. He took off and we headed back to the border and right through customs with an empty car.

+

At 2:30 a.m. on February 24, 2004, within a week of the arrest, a severe earthquake struck the Moroccan city of Al Hoceima about ninety miles west of Melilla. Within a matter of minutes, twelve thousand homes were completely leveled and a proportionate number of people killed. In a region where construction entails little more than stones stacked on top of one another, even a small earthquake can cause severe damage. The 6.3 that struck in the middle of that night proved to be catastrophic for the surrounding villages. Almost all of the Moroccan villagers in the region had been left without food and shelter.

I was in Melilla when the earthquake struck. We felt the tremors, but nothing was damaged and no one was hurt. We had no idea what was happening just to our west. That evening I got a phone call from Paul who was in England on business. He had heard about the serious situation in Al Hoceima. He was going to wire me $5,000 the following morning; I was to fill the van with blankets and food and go to Al Hoceima. We had a couple of partners in that city who knew the region well.

The scene that awaited me in Al Hoceima was horrific. Homes were destroyed, huge concrete buildings had collapsed with people still trapped inside. Men with pickaxes stood on top, chipping away at mountains of rubble. Every standing structure was completely deserted. People had moved into the fields and streets, as far away from the buildings as they could get. Some were rioting, setting up roadblocks and stopping to loot trucks full of supplies. Insanity prevailed.

All of a sudden the ground shook again and everyone screamed and ran from the street into the fields. It was another aftershock measuring about 5 on the Richter scale. These were a common occurrence in the days immediately after the earthquake.

Most of the buildings that had been built using concrete and rebar were unaffected by the earthquake. The true devastation was just outside of the cities, in the villages scattered throughout the mountains. I was headed to a gated complex in the middle of the city where our partners had gathered and begun distributing the much needed supplies into the countryside. I arrived in the evening with Paul's van still in one piece and immediately joined the effort.

For the next several days we traveled into the remote villages nestled into the Riff mountain range of northern Morocco, the first to bring aid to dozens of villages in the days after the earthquake. The Moroccan news even did a story on us asking the question, "Why is it these American Christians were the first ones to help our own people?" The Moroccan government had announced that the earthquake's death toll was six hundred people, but as we kept traveling into more and more villages it became apparent that this number was nowhere near the actual total. And the damage was much worse than anyone realized.

For the next three weeks I lived in Al Hoceima. Every family in the countryside had lost someone. Every home was destroyed. An entire region—tens of thousands of people—had lost all they owned overnight. In the moment, my focus was on meeting the needs, nothing else. But eventually the immediate need was met and I had time, dreaded time, to sit and to think—to let my mind wander.

All of the tragedy of the past month was starting to take its toll on me. For eight months I had looked into the eyes of dying men on the mountain of Gurugu and told most of them that there was nothing I could do to help them. Then, in a day, the good that I *was* doing was abruptly ended and those whom

I had grown to care about the most were the victims. Just three days later the earthquake hit and I was once again right in the middle of a disaster. I was trying to help people who had lost so much, but no amount of love or goodwill can bring back a dead family member. Houses can be rebuilt, but once destroyed, homes are never the same. The hills were filled with hundreds of fresh graves. Dead and rotting animal carcasses littered the countryside. The whole place stunk of death.

When tragedy strikes on such a grand scale all at once, a strange thing happens. The very earth itself becomes devoid of hope and joy and an eerie emptiness remains from which there is no escape. It's like being stuck in a box. You can move, shifting the pain from one spot to another, but you can't stand up. You can't get away. Once it consumes you, there is no relief. My heart was with the people in Al Hoceima, my heart was with the refugees—and it was tearing me apart. I started to wonder how anyone could do this work and have a heart at all.

Exhausted, I returned to Melilla.

Spain didn't feel nearly as warm and welcoming as it once had. My roommate, Diego, had a pot of spaghetti waiting for me when I got back to my house. He didn't ask me a thing about Al Hoceima. He didn't need to—he could see how heavily it weighed on me.

I needed to clear my head. I went for a run and tried to work out at the gym. All of my Spanish friends were there and excitedly welcomed me back. They all wanted to hear stories about the earthquake. I didn't much feel like talking about it. One of the guys trying to cheer me up asked me if I had "nailed any good Moroccan broads." Another wanted to know if I had seen a lot of dead people, as if it were some cool thing.

I turned around and began to walk.

I continued to wander in a bit of a daze for two months. I don't particularly know what filled that time. I had no project to support, no cause to embrace. I did attempt to make trips to the refugee camp, but every time I was followed up the mountain and arrested by the Moroccans when I tried to cross the border back into Spain. As a result, I ended up in jail four more times. Finally I gave up after being told that I would be forever exiled from Morocco if I was ever seen in Morocco with a black man or anywhere near Gurugu again.

I continued to work out. I hung out with my Spanish friends. I spent a lot of time alone down by the ocean. I took a couple trips traveling through Spain. I filled each day with any number of meaningless tasks to speed the clock along. I was scheduled to go home for a month at the end of May to raise support and be with my family. That was my goal, my destination. I wanted nothing more than for the time to pass so I could take a break and return to the comfort of home. On the outside I remained the optimistic, outgoing guy I had always been. No one truly knew how much what I had seen and done plagued me.

Together with Manolo, we had helped so many on Gurugu. That effort had to continue despite the Moroccans' warnings, but at the same time we weren't solving the deepest problems of the refugees, just treating symptoms. The roots of what we saw on Gurugu were buried in sub-Saharan and west Africa. I had to know more. I wanted to make a difference in Africa, but awareness always precedes progress. I needed to see and experience Africa with my own eyes. The stories my refugee friends told me weren't enough.

I began to explore the possibility of a journey through several of the central African countries. When problems arose almost immediately, I knew I was on the right track. I was searching for something adventurous, something that had never been done before. It was perfect.

Many of the places my refugee friends had fled had very little if any infrastructure, let alone reliable public transportation. If a journey through these countries was going to be possible, I would need my own transportation. But even if I could somehow acquire visas to all of these countries, roads were not always available. Even the most detailed maps I could find of western Tanzania, eastern Democratic Republic of Congo, and northern Kenya offered only speculated routes of local trade, likely nothing more than dirt paths through the jungle. I would need an all-terrain vehicle that was tough enough to withstand anything. In my twenty-one-year-old, testosterone-marinated mind only one option seemed reasonable: a dirt bike.

I called two of my best lifelong buddies and it didn't take much convincing for them to catch the vision and agree to join me. I arrived home, and with renewed energy and excitement, my friends and I began to plan the trip of a lifetime—beginning a journey that ended so much differently than we ever expected.

Welcome to Hell

Cairo, Egypt

A flash. Pain. The sun explodes and I'm airborne. But then I land, twenty feet away, and I realize the earth is still intact. I can't move. The choking smell of gunpowder fills my lungs and a high-pitched scream assaults me from inside my head, blocking out every other sound. I can see people screaming and running. Slowly the commotion starts to make sense to me and I hear someone yell my name.

"Erik! Where's Erik?" It's my brother's voice. He's okay. He's looking for me.

I scream for him, but get no response. Next to me a demolished moped smolders. Body parts lie on the ground all around me.

A man runs over with a fire extinguisher.

Can this be a dream? I know it's not. Dreams don't hurt like this. What's happened? Where are my friends? Where is my brother?

I scream again. "ALEX! ALEX!" But he doesn't answer. I'm alone with the ringing in my head and muffled screams in a language I can't understand.

I try to get up. God, it hurts. My whole body is on fire. My legs won't move and the back of my left arm is blown apart. I reach with my right hand to feel the damage. Wet bone is the first thing I feel where my triceps used to be. Blood is everywhere. I wonder how much of it is mine. I'm losing it fast. I wonder how long I have before I go unconscious.

I can't go unconscious—I have to find my brother.

I look down and see that I am naked. The explosion blew off everything but the collar of my shirt and my belt. Hundreds of nails are sticking out of my legs. I feel the back of my head with my bloody right hand—only to discover more nails.

This is shrapnel. The burning moped didn't cause this. This is no accident. Someone wanted this. Someone purposely brought this hell to earth.

"Alex!" I yell weakly. "Kris! Mike!" Are they alive? Am I alive? It hurts too much for me to be dead. I'm losing a lot of blood. How much longer do I have?

It can't end like this. We've come so far.

Just hold on. Fight ... you can't die yet.

I look around me; the smoke is starting to clear. A layer of broken glass and little pieces of wood cover the street. A crowd is gathering. Why are they just watching? *Help us!* Why are they just looking?

I see Alex. Thank God he's alive. I can't yell anymore. Did he hear me before? I don't have the strength to yell again.

He is just lying there all alone. His head is moving. He looks conscious. I can see he is in immense pain. I muster up my last reserve: "Hold on, buddy. Help will be here soon. Just hold on."

I see Kris. He's alive! He's on the other side of the narrow street. His face is black except for the red streams running from it to his chest below. He is holding his left arm; it's full of holes. Looks like a pincushion. He stumbles around. I can tell by looking at him that he can't see very well.

"Kris!" I say as loudly as I can manage.

He stops and turns toward me. He's no more than ten feet away now. He squints and comes and kneels beside me.

"Go to Alex. Make sure he is okay," I wince. If there were any way at all that I could have gone to Alex myself, I would have been beside him already. Kris knows that. He looks at my body, at the river of blood flowing from me down the stone street. Even through the burns and blood, I can tell he is afraid for me. He knows my time is short.

But I don't care about that. Alex is all that matters.

I can only imagine what must be running through Alex's head as Kris tends to him. Riddled deep throughout his body are hundreds of nails. The nails in his chest and waist are all aligned horizontally. Further down, the nails point down and to the left. His left cheekbone is broken, his face severely burnt, his eye cut. The outside of his left leg is severely burned and blown apart, and his foot is missing two toes. He was just a couple feet away from the bomb when it went off, but he doesn't look much worse than Kris or me.

But then he speaks: "Tell my mom and dad I love them."

"Quit talking like that," Kris says. "We've been in tight spots before. You fight. We'll pull through this. Erik is doing great; don't worry about him. You're going to be okay too."

I begin to pull the nails out of my leg. From where I am, it hurts to look behind me to my brother. It hurts to sit. It hurts to breathe. I am losing more blood and am starting to get cold.

Kris comes back and tells me that Alex is alive and that I have it worse than he does. "He's only semiconscious, but I think he'll be okay," Kris tells me.

Oh thank God. If I can stay alive, then I know he'll be able to.

Kris and I each have one working arm. Together we take a shirt and tie a tourniquet around my arm and leg to slow the bleeding. My left leg feels like every bone between my knee and toes is shattered. My skin is blown off most of my butt and legs, but my back feels okay. I had been wearing a backpack, I remember. That must have taken some of the impact. I look and see the shredded backpack full of nails another three feet from me. I reach for it and take out my passport and lay it on my chest.

Kris and I start to pray. "Please, God, save us. Who could do this terrible thing? Please God, let Alex live. Please God, let Mike be alive."

Where is Mike?

There is a leg lying right next to me. "Oh, God." My soul gasps as our hearts drop even deeper to a place that no one should know. This place. This hell, my new home. I won't be leaving this place anytime soon. We reach out toward our best friend's left leg, severed above the knee. Kris looks at me with tears in his eyes.

Is this Mike? Please, God, don't let this be Mike.

This can't be Mike. Mike was wearing sandals; this leg is wearing a black sock. *The bomber?* I look away in disgust and nearly vomit.

There is nothing to do now but wait. I send Kris to be with Alex. He will take care of my dear brother.

An eternity passes before the first ambulance comes. Kris makes sure that Alex is taken first. Kris knows I would never get on the ambulance before my brother, no matter how bad off I was. I see them drive away. I am so relieved. Alex is going to be okay; he is being taken care of.

I look again at the size of the pool of blood around me and lay down, waiting to go unconscious or to slip into shock. Kris comes back to my side, assuring me that Alex is going to be just fine, but there is still no sign of Mike. No one will say it, but we both know deep down that he's dead. I pull a pink blanket over my naked, bloody body and wait.

Another eternity passes.

I don't go unconscious.

I wish I could but I don't.

Another ambulance comes. Kris is running and shouting at the paramedics. The stretcher comes for me. *"Wahed, juje, thlata."* I'm on the stretcher. Kris is still shouting; he's all I can hear over the ringing in my head.

I find myself in the back of an ambulance with a dead woman next to me. Kris is trying to shut the door to the ambulance. He is still shouting at them to go.

One man is frantically grabbing my stretcher and yelling; he is trying to pull me off the ambulance! With his good arm Kris shoves the man in the chest, then puts himself between the man and my stretcher. "I will kill you," he shouts, "if you try to take my friend off of this ambulance." He means it.

The man can't understand the words, but there is no mistaking what has just been communicated.

"Rip that throat right out of your neck and kill you," Kris snarls.

The man stands back. Kris will not let him near.

They pile another corpse on top of me. Finally the ambulance starts to move.

Is this the end?

We had traveled over nine thousand miles through eleven of the world's darkest and most mysterious countries, through hundreds of different tribes and languages. We had survived two different civil wars, five different rebel factions, countless man-eating animals, hunger, breakdowns, and armed bandits.

Our team of brothers had lived when anyone else would have died. We had braved the fiercest dangers, assured that we were living the lives we had been created to live, and had successfully reached our destination.

Now after having completed our journey, with two leisure weeks left as regular tourists, all seems lost. I had trusted God and followed his plan — and ended up in hell.

Proud boys with their bikes (left to right: me, Alex, and Kris).

NO TURNING BACK
Somewhere over Africa

Four months earlier, three almost new KLR 650 duel sport motorcycles sat in an airfreight terminal in Michigan while Alex, Kris, and I buzzed through the sky somewhere over the massive continent of Africa. Alex stared in awe out his window over the vast sea of green below. "I can't believe how huge this continent is. Look at the jungle; it stretches as far as you can see in every direction."

I leaned over my brother, whose seat was closest to the window. "So this is what Africa looks like on the other side of the desert." I was looking for a road, a trail, any trace of humanity. We were going to travel back through these same forests on our dirt bikes in another two months. The nervous excitement began to bubble up in my chest. I took a deep breath and grabbed Alex's shoulders. He couldn't hold back his grin.

Hour after hour the plane sped over the endless mass of land. Our destination, Cape Town, South Africa, still seemed forever away.

"What's Kris doing?" I saw him upfront tampering with the lavatory door handle. He looked up at us nervously and came back to his seat, which was just in front of Alex and me. He was laughing.

"Did you break something?" Alex asked.

"Yeah, I tried to open the door and the stupid handle pulled right off!"

"You know it's a push door, right?"

"Well, yeah, I do now."

"Did you fix it?" Alex asked.

"Of course he fixed it. Kris always fixes it."

"Of course I fixed it."

We started a game of cards as we discussed the journey ahead. We were too wired to sleep. Each of us knew that every moment we spent in that plane speeding through the sky meant hours of grueling jungle trails. Every mile we continued further we would have to retrace on our dirt bikes.

We had been talking about this trip for almost a year now—ever since Africa had first captured my heart.

Alex, though, was never supposed to be a part of this crazy plan. He was my little brother, and I didn't want to risk putting him in a dangerous situation that I wouldn't be able to get him out of—and I knew that this journey would be perilous. My life was something I would risk, if needed. I would put myself in harm's way if the situation called for it. I had done it before with the refugees, and I would do it again for my friends. But Alex, he was precious to me, and the thought of him being injured or worse was unbearable. Besides, when we first started making plans, Alex was still just a seventeen-year-old kid finishing high school. He hadn't had the chance to have his courage and perseverance truly tested and proven. I didn't know if he would be able to cut it. Hunger, cold, fear, and exhaustion were all guaranteed.

But things were different now. During his senior year of high school while I was in Melilla, Alex decided that he too wanted a taste of life outside the US. He wanted to learn languages and cultures and help people in need. Over the last months of school he made plans to move to the Andalusian city of Malaga to study Spanish during the summer before college. Malaga was just an eight-hour boat ride away from Melilla, where I was living. Though still not on the same continent, we would be living the closest we had been in three years.

While he was making that decision, I was getting ready to return home from my first year in Africa. I had imagined my homecoming a thousand times, stepping off the plane and walking through the familiar Grand Rapids airport. I could even smell it. The air would rush over the great lake, drift through a string of green grassy fields, and find its way into my lungs. There wouldn't be even a hint of danger or hunger in it. I would walk off the plane to find my loved ones ready to welcome me, proudly congratulating me. I would step into the comfortable, loving refuge that was home and enjoy the life I was so lucky to have.

I had gone over the scene so many times in my head I almost began to wonder if the whole thing was made up, a figment of my hopes. The airport, my white house with brown shingles, my healthy happy family, and my little white spotted dog—none of these things even seemed real to me anymore. They were so far removed from where I had been. They seemed to exist in an entirely different realm, one that was ignorant to the sufferings of this world.

Going to Morocco—experiencing the refugees and living with the earthquake victims—was kind of like jumping into a frozen lake. By now the shock had worn off, but I was slowly freezing to death. Still, would going home be worse? I was about to hop into a hot tub, and that transition could be more painful than the cold.

My homecoming was just as I had imagined it would be. All of my family and friends were so proud of me. I had journeyed to the ends of the earth and found my place. I had helped save lives. I had made a difference. I had been tested and proven strong. Alex was the first to embrace me. My parents weren't far behind. It had been only a year that I had been away, but it felt like so much longer. When I had left that very airport just one year earlier, I was a boy who believed there was more to life than selfish pursuits. I was returning a man who had courageously embraced his destiny. I was tired, but I had made it back. I was home at last.

Home was the same as I had left it. Familiar. It smelled the same; it looked the same. The same faces walked up and down the same streets. It offered all the same comforts that it used to. Yet I was thoroughly unsettled. I spent time with my friends, but I quickly discovered that I didn't have much to talk with them about. I didn't have much to say to anybody. All of the conversations seemed so petty. Their praise seemed nothing more than pretense. They thought that I was a hero, but I sure didn't feel like one. A hero wouldn't have taken a month and hundreds of dollars to indulge his own personal comfort, not to mention ego. Sure, I had helped a lot of people and that was a great thing, but the truth was that most of those people were still suffering right now as I sat in comfort. When I returned to Morocco next month, how many more refugees would have been shot and killed? How many of the sick would have died? How many of the healthy would have fallen ill? The homeless in Al Hoceima would still be homeless.

I knew this, but my American friends didn't. Their lack of knowledge didn't change the truth; neither did my knowledge.

The difference was that I felt accountable for something about which they were completely ignorant. They were free to go about their lives oblivious to what my friends in Africa were enduring, to what people all over the world had to endure.

Again I managed to keep my frustrations buried. I reverted to a mindless college student. I went to parties, I watched movies, and I gorged on American pop culture. Everyone who knew me during this time would have told you that I was doing great. Almost no one noticed how distanced I was — no one except my perceptive little brother, no one but Alex.

I spent a lot of time with Alex during my month home. The month started rough, but gradually, without me even realizing, our conversation shifted from my frustration to excitement about the months to come. Besides, I was home to watch him graduate. I was there at his open house. I got to watch the end of his track season. He was the team captain and finished fifth in the state in the pole vault. I was in the audience a couple weeks later at the high school's athletic banquet when he was presented the Pat Paterson Memorial Award, a trophy for outstanding athletic ability, leadership, and character, awarded to only one athlete each year. It was the very award I had received three years earlier. I was gleaming with pride. He had not only survived high school, but he had thrived. He had challenged himself and had come out on top. That night we put his trophy on the mantel next to mine. His was fresh and shiny; mine had started to dull and chip — but they stood side by side.

And then came the day we left that all behind — an invincible team, bonded by more than brotherhood. We stepped off the plane in the Malaga airport. The sea breeze greeted us and the sunshine warmed my shoulders. It was a very different place than I had left only a month earlier. I was seeing it through refreshed eyes.

Alex was beaming. Such a radical change was scary at any age, and at just eighteen years old he would be doing it all alone, without the guiding footsteps of parents or teachers. Even I would be a continent away. But he was ready whether he knew it yet or not.

✦

After a couple weeks exploring the sights together, I headed back through Melilla to Al Hoceima to help rebuild the homes that were destroyed in the earthquake four months earlier. The work was long, hot, sweaty, and tough. I loved it.

At the end of the summer, the earthquake relief project supervisor was due back in the States for a few months. Originally he planned to put the work in Al Hoceima on hold while he was away, but he and Paul both seemed convinced that I could handle the entire project on my own. I was excited about the responsibility. I knew that I could do it, but it wasn't going to be easy. I would need help.

At that very moment, my brother was on a boat headed to Melilla. We hadn't seen each other in three weeks—ever since a weekend together in Pamplona—and no matter how busy I was, I was going to take a couple days off to spend time with him. This would almost certainly be the last time I would see him before he went back to the States.

He looked taller and stronger, noticeably older. It was crazy. We had been apart for less than a month but something was different. It wasn't that his physical features had changed any. The difference was in his poise. He carried himself with a confidence, a humble strength that before that day I had seen only glimpses of. Now he wore it as if it were his skin.

We went straight back to my buddy Diego's house, where I had a room, and began catching up. He had been waiting to tell me about school and new friends and all the Spanish he was learning, though he was much more reluctant to actually speak Spanish. There was one story he was particularly proud of.

"So the other day we're sitting in class and the class conversation gets on sex and everyone starts talking about what they like and who they're sleeping with. Eventually they asked me what I think. I told them that I didn't sleep around and that honestly I wasn't looking for anyone to bring home that night. The whole class was stunned and they all started giving me a hard time. Then I told them that I'm a virgin and I think that sex is a big deal and should be saved for the girl you're going to spend your life with."

"No kidding," I interjected. "You stood your ground in front of the whole class, huh?"

"Right, so then after class every single one of the people who was giving me a hard time in front of the class comes up to me and says that they really respected what I had to say and that I had the guts to stand up for it."

"You're kidding me."

"Nope. Every single one."

"I tell you what, little brother. I couldn't cruise the topless beaches of southern Spain and stand by my convictions like you are."

"Maybe that's why you ended up in Morocco?"

I couldn't help but laugh. Maybe he was right. My brother was living the life I had found the hard way but with none of my scars.

It was my turn to share. I told him about the situation in Al Hoceima and the work that I would be doing. I told him about my recent promotion to "head honcho" of the project. That same stupid grin that I was wearing a moment earlier found its way to Alex's face.

"Good for you, Erik" he said proudly. "You're going to do a great job."

"About that, Alex. Here's a thought for you. So you're scheduled to fly back to the States and start college in what, two weeks?"

"Yeah ..." he said in a disappointed but probing tone.

"Well, I was thinking ... I am going to need a partner in Al Hoceima. I have a lot to do and I can't do it alone. What if you don't get on that plane?"

The grin exploded into laughter. "Ahh, yeah, I was thinking about that myself."

"Mom's gonna freak out."

"She's gonna love it."

+

Alex and I were born and raised the only two children in a divorced family. We spent our childhood bouncing back and forth from one household to the other. We spent the majority of our early lives with our lovely mom; her house has always been my home. With our mom, Alex and I had a lot of freedom. She had to work full time to support us, so from a very early age we were responsible for getting up in the morning, getting off to school, and taking care of ourselves in the afternoons. Such freedom was great for two naughty boys and afforded us plenty of opportunity to get into trouble. I remember one time Alex and his friend made a life-size trebuchet in the backyard and launched my weight set over three hundred feet through our neighbors' backyards. He was in sixth grade at the time.

Then not a year later he constructed a combustion-driven fireball cannon. To the uninformed observer his device looked like a harmless piece of nine-foot PVC pipe, but when the proper attachments were added and the right ingredients were put into place, it turned lethal. I'll never forget the much anticipated test day when a bunch of neighborhood kids had gathered to see the spectacle. Alex ignited the first round. BOOM! An eight-inch flaming ball fired uncontrollably hundreds of feet through the air before landing on our trampoline and setting it on fire. We all rushed to put it out, but not before it had burnt through the mat.

"Wow!" the crowd exclaimed. "Do it again."

Alex looked at me.

"Yeah, do it again."

BOOM! Another round went off and landed dangerously close to the house—right as our mom opened the sliding door to see what the ruckus was. She quickly, with more than a few words, put an end to our destructive fun. When asked why I, the older and more mature of the two, didn't stop this idiotic stunt I replied, "It seemed like a good idea. Did you see the air that ball gets?"

Alex and I spent every other weekend and Wednesday nights with our dad. He was much firmer in his approach to parenting. A mindless stunt like the fireball cannon would bring a good scorn from Mom, but if Dad had ever caught us doing something like that I doubt that I would be here to write this story. My dad's firmness didn't really stop us from being troublesome kids, it just taught us how to not get caught.

Growing up was tough. We never knew who we would spend Christmas with or where we would be sleeping at night, and we had to deal with the emotional rollercoaster that a divorce will put any loving parent on. But as a result of this imperfect childhood, my brother and I bonded in a way that would never have been possible in any other circumstance. Early on in our lives we could count on very little consistency, but the one thing that we could always count on was that we would be together no matter what. Regardless of what happened, we always had each other.

A month after I graduated from high school, I got on a plane and left Grand Rapids. That was over three years ago, and in that whole time not a week had gone by that we hadn't talked. And here we were back together again.

Alex changed his flight and his whole plan for fall semester.

"College will be there in another six months. I want to do something really important first," was all he would say when concerned adults asked if this was the wisest life decision.

Neither of our parents was even a little bit surprised by the change of plan. All they said was, "I saw this coming."

But even after all that, I wasn't ready to let him come on the bike trip through the wildest heart of Africa.

One day, Alex sat me down after a long day of working in the hot African sun and said, "Erik, you are going on the trip of a lifetime. You will never do anything like this again, and I will never have the opportunity to do anything like this again because no one else I know would attempt it. Even if they did, I wouldn't go because there is no one else I trust enough to do something like this with. You will remember this journey and tell stories about it for the rest of your life, and I want to be a part of it. I want to come with you."

I knew he was right. My brother was no longer a boy who needed to be looked after. He had revealed the strong, confident, capable, and courageous man that he was becoming every day. I knew he was as capable as I was to deal with any problems that may arise. I knew that he could make it as well as any of us. He was no longer my little brother just begging to tag along. He was a man telling me that his rightful place was beside me.

Again, neither of our parents was surprised by the news that we would be attempting this journey together and neither ever tried to talk us out of it. But a million details needed to be worked out before we could call this anything more than a crazy idea.

We needed support along the way. I started calling and emailing many humanitarian workers with whom I had indirectly become acquainted over the past several months and asked them about different projects going on in Africa. Those with projects we could actually contribute to found their way into a stack of contacts. We bought a wall-size map of Africa; every potential contact received a small spot of duct tape with a number on it. Eventually we connected the dots, and a trail through some of the world's most desperate and mysterious countries, starting in South Africa and stretching over nine thousand miles north to Egypt, revealed itself.

Getting reliable information about the places we wanted to go was next to impossible, especially from the remote villages that we were living in. Internet, where available, was mind-numbingly slow and phones were ridiculously expensive. Alex and I communicated with Kris and Mike every couple of weeks.

We decided that we would start our journey at the beginning of January 2005, after Alex and I had fulfilled our commitment with Partnerships International in north Africa. Mike was finishing up four years of service with the Air Force and wasn't sure exactly what date he would be discharged; he promised to meet up with us wherever we were along the way as soon as he was able. We would take about four months to traverse Africa before flying home on April 22, my brother's nineteenth birthday.

✦

After Alex and I had fulfilled our responsibilities in north Africa and said good-bye to our dear friends, we returned home to Grand Rapids for a month. Normally a trip like this would take years to plan; we had three weeks before we had to get back on a plane.

We needed to find stallions worthy of the journey and needed to stock up on enough spare parts to get us through the breakdowns that were sure to come. We would have to carry in everything we would need to keep our bikes running as there would be no hope of resupplying en route. We would have no chase vehicle like they have in the Paris-Dakar. We were going to be completely on our own across the rugged miles of untamed desert, jungle, and rainforest.

We found three reliable, affordable dirt bikes. It turned out that it was actually cheaper to buy the motorcycles in the States and ship them over and back than to buy the same three bikes in South Africa. Plus having our bikes exported only temporarily from the US made the legalities of transiting through many of the African countries much simpler. Kris and Alex were both pretty handy with engines, so they took charge of supplying our tools and spare parts while I started researching what needed to be worked out in order for us to travel through these countries.

Three weeks later, after countless phone calls and several loans, we were ready to go. An international shipping company had picked up our motorcycles and was scheduled to deliver them to Cape Town a week after we landed. We had managed to obtain an international Carnet du Passage, which was basically a passport for the vehicles. This handy little piece of paper would let us pass through almost any country in Africa without having to pay import taxes. Goofy with excitement, we bought one-way tickets to Cape Town. We got traveler's health insurance and packed three duffel bags with all of the gear we could possibly need—a load of spare parts, a sleeping bag, some extra underwear, and a couple of walkie-talkies—which we could easily strap to the back of our bikes.

And here we were, flying over the great Africa. There could be no second-guessing, no turning back. We had pulled it off. We had actually gotten everything done and now we were sitting like three little boys on Christmas morning, thirty-five thousand feet over the continent that had captured my heart. This was where the voice within had led me.

I looked at Alex and Kris who were admiring the view. I wouldn't trust anyone else in the world more than these two men, no one else with whom I would attempt this trip. We were together, we were a team, and nothing could stop us.

I stared out the window along with them. The hum of the engines was almost hypnotic and our destination approached.

THE TESTING BEGINS

South Africa

Three happy little children who lived near Josie.

The sun had long since set by the time our plane touched down. We were waiting for our baggage in the Cape Town airport. Kris broke out the deck of cards and we prepared ourselves for yet another game of three-man rummy. Alex was sprawled out on the floor, his head propped against his carry-on backpack, reading brochures of things to see and do in South Africa. Kris dealt.

"Are we going to drive along the Garden Route?" Alex asked.

"Huh?"

"'Cause we should; it looks pretty cool."

"Sure. Hey, it's your turn."

Alex sat up and grabbed his cards. "Yeah, it's this highway that travels along the southern coast of South Africa. It's supposed to be beautiful. We should when we finish here in Cape Town."

Kris leaned over and looked at the brochure. I asked a guy walking by what was taking so long.

"Oh, your bags didn't make it on the flight. You need to talk to the people behind the desk."

"I'll be back in a minute, guys." Neither of them looked up; they were both looking at the brochure now.

A few minutes later I came back. They had finished with the brochure and were trying to negotiate their game of rummy without me.

"Well, our bags aren't coming for a couple days, but the good news is that they are giving us 350 rand (about $50) per bag that didn't make it. That'll cover a cab out of here and a room for tonight. You boys ready to roll?"

They stood up and we grabbed the stuff we did have. We didn't have any plans for the night and it was almost midnight. We caught a cab and asked the driver to take us to the closest hostel.

We were tired but thrilled. We had made it. We were actually in South Africa about to embark on the journey of a lifetime. Life was good. None of us had a hard time falling asleep that night.

⌖

The next morning we called our first contact, a wonderfully gracious couple named Jenneta and Willem. Our bags had arrived earlier than expected and were waiting for us at the airport. After reclaiming our gear, they invited us into their home as if we were family and showed us around the Cape.

Post-apartheid South Africa is a unique place. Officially the institutionalized racial discrimination that was apartheid had been abolished for over a decade. New laws and a new government had been put in place, guaranteeing legal equality for all colors and creeds. But socially and economically the chasm that separated the white minority from the black majority remained. At first glance this tension was easy to miss. Cape Town was a nice city, like a little piece of Europe hidden under Africa. Jenneta and Willem lived on the outskirts of Cape Town in a town called Stellenbosch, the heart of South Africa's wine country. As we drove through the beautiful rolling vineyards it was easy to forget that we were even in Africa. It looked more like Napa, California.

Yet stuck right in the middle of all this luxury and beauty were the shantytowns—one of many scars apartheid left. The people who lived in the shantytowns experienced a totally different reality than the white Afrikaners. An invisible, impassable line still existed. The blacks were poor; the blacks didn't own cars; the blacks didn't go wine-and-cheese tasting—and most of the whites lived complacently convinced that all was well.

Our hosts and the people they worked with were some of the exceptions. Willem worked with a church in a shantytown trying to help develop AIDS awareness and care for the youth. He took us into one of the shantytowns and gave us a list of projects that needed to be done. For a couple of days we labored alongside black men our age, working to help improve their communities.

The younger children seemed to naturally gravitate toward Alex. They were absolutely adorable; they ran around with muddy faces and begged you to carry them. It was hard to go anywhere without one of these little guys in your arms and another holding your free hand. Sadly, about half of them were born with HIV.

One day we were digging a garden alongside the church-owned community center located on the periphery of the shantytown. It was so overgrown that it looked like it hadn't been cared for in years. I looked over at Alex. He was breaking up the ground with a spade. A little boy no more than five, struggling with a hoe way too big for him, was trying to help. Kris was working the shovel while I raked out the weeds.

We didn't travel far into the shantytown. Our projects were all on the edge—and frankly we had no business proceeding any further. But we became friends with some of the young men who lived there, and we were curious. "What's it like back in your community, back in the shanties? What's it like where you sleep?" I asked Josie, one of the young men.

He hesitated. "It's a different place I think than what you are used to," he replied, looking down at the pile of weeds in front of him.

A brief but awkward silence passed.

He looked up at us. "You should come stay with me tonight."

The other black workers all agreed. "Yeah, come stay with us. It's Friday night . . . we will have a good time," someone else offered.

Kris and Alex both looked at me and without a word told me to take him up on his invitation.

"We'd love to."

All of our fellow workers smiled and turned back to the garden. We had a lot to do before anything but weeds would grow in that mess.

✦

That evening after we finished the day's work, we followed Josie back into the shantytown. The shacks were no more than fifteen-foot-wide squares stacked so close together that a rat could barely fit between them. Each housed between two and ten people. As we walked deeper into the shantytown I felt more and more eyes follow us. We three white boys were all tight together just behind Josie.

Alex leaned over to me. "Do you feel like we're really not welcome here? I'm getting a pretty bad vibe from most of these people."

“Maybe this wasn’t such a great idea,” I responded, but we all knew it was too late to do anything about it now. We weren’t going to get picked up until the following day and we didn’t have a cell phone.

We looked out to the road. Semitrucks full of beer were unloading their cargo while men ran out to the street clutching the few bucks they had been able to earn that week.

“The men here, they like to drink some beer on the Friday and Saturday nights,” Josie explained. “It’s a big problem ’cause a lot of the children don’t have no food ’cause their papas spend the money on the beer.”

One of the church’s volunteers had told us that they regularly found dead babies in the forest surrounding the shantytown. Moms just couldn’t take care of them so they left them to die. The orphanages were full of babies that had been found in dumpsters. Crime was rampant in these communities as well. Brawls often turned lethal.

Next to one of the trucks I saw a man sitting on the chest of another man, pounding the broken, bloody, half conscious face with his fists. A group casually watched as people continued by, paying little attention to the scene.

I looked at Alex as he was watching the situation unfold. “Alex,” I whispered.

Nothing.

“Alex!”

He was still gaping.

“ALEX!”

“Huh, what?” He looked like he was going to throw up.

I knew he wanted to go over there. I could tell he wanted to do something. Before he had a chance to think or say anything, I interrupted him. "Hey, keep moving. Let's go."

Kris moved over toward him and urged him along. "Come on, Alex."

We finally arrived at a shack no different than the thousand others we passed before it. Inside were all the guys we had been working with the past two days. They welcomed us warmly. Eight of us jammed into this shack no bigger than a toolshed and more humbly built. The conversation was primarily in Zulu.

We sat sipping on ginger soda ignorant to the nature of the conversation until Josie motioned that it was time to leave. We followed him back to his shack. Josie was one of the few in the community who lived alone, though given his "spacious" living situation he often had guests. He had sided his home with scraps of sun-faded wood he was able to find; the roof was just one sheet of tin; the open space in the wall was a glassless window. The temperature inside had to be a hundred degrees. Josie flung open the makeshift shutters, letting in a cool breeze. The shack was no bigger than a closet, with a small bed jammed on one side and a tight area where two or three people could stand on the other.

"Hey, Josie, where do we go if we need to use the bathroom?"

"We got a toilet close by. We should go now."

He grabbed an old key on a pink plastic string and we followed him out the door through a claustrophobic alley. We could smell the stench before we could see the bathrooms. We turned one last corner to see a concrete structure with a half dozen steel doors. Josie fitted his key into one of them and turned the door open. A wave of urine-soaked air hit us. It was hard to breathe.

"How many people do you share this with, Josie?"

"Oh, there are about thirty other people who use this toilet."

Alex stepped in and relieved himself. I was next.

We ended up back in Josie's shack. I slept in the bed with him; Alex and Kris were lying close by on the floor.

This was how Josie slept every night; this was how he lived every day.

I tried to sleep. I was tired but it was so hot.

+

Our first week passed quickly with Jenneta and Willem. Finally came the day our bikes were scheduled to arrive. Kris kicked off the morning by jumping up on his bed in his underwear and singing his own rendition of "Life Is a Highway." Alex wasn't far behind on backup vocals. I just assaulted them both by throwing dirty socks until they stopped singing, took cover, and returned fire. We were excited for our bikes to come.

I called the airfreight terminal to check on the status of our shipment.

"Bikes?" they said. "What bikes?"

I knew they had to be there—we had called the shipping company a week earlier and they had assured us of the bikes' timely arrival.

"Dirt bikes!" I said. "Three of them! Tell me you're kidding."

"So sorry, sir. We have no dirt bikes coming in the month of January."

I got the shipping company on the phone. "Ah, yes," I was told. "Apparently the person working with you forgot to give you a piece of paperwork to sign. Could you come in to sign it so we could get your shipment out?"

"I'm on the other side of the world, where my bikes are supposed to be," I said loudly. "I can't come in to sign anything!"

Alex and Kris were watching me anxiously.

"I'm afraid we can't make the shipment, then, sir. I am very sorry."

We wrested a bit longer on the phone, but to no avail. I hung up and groaned. Our only means of transportation was still sitting in Detroit with no promise of being delivered to Cape Town anytime soon.

Alex and I called our dad. He heard the situation and said only, "I'll take care of it. You guys enjoy South Africa. I'll call you tomorrow." That was it.

The following day the phone rang and our dad was on the other end of the line. "Your bikes will be there in a few days."

"What? How did you do that? Are you sure?" Alex was incredulous.

"Well, it wasn't all that easy but don't worry about it. They'll be there soon."

With his assurance that the bikes were coming, we all slept soundly that night.

A week later our bikes did come. I don't know if anything could compare to that moment we first saw the big wooden container just as we had left it in Michigan a few weeks earlier. We attacked it with hammers and crowbars, ripping the wood off like three kids racing to unwrap their birthday presents. There they were: three beautiful 650cc dirt bikes, our stallions, ready to carry us anywhere we were willing to go. We rolled them out of their container across the warehouse to our pile of tools. They each fired right up on the first try, as anxious as we were to start this journey.

We thanked Jenneta and Willem for their hospitality and bid them farewell. We were off—three men, three bikes, three duffel bags.

All the worries of the past couple weeks—the uncertainty, the anxiety—lifted off my shoulders as we climbed the highway over the pass, out of the valley, out of Cape Town. For two weeks I had looked at this road. Now we were driving over it. It was just a couple hours along Alex's spectacular Garden Route to the southern most tip of Africa where the Atlantic and the Indian oceans meet. The three of us stood there together and looked south. Antarctica was just beyond the horizon. We turned and looked north. The whole continent of Africa lay ahead of us ready to share her endless secrets and mysteries. We were ready.

⌖

Our first destination was Johannesburg, some eight hundred and forty miles to the north. We still needed to pick up a couple visas, and Joburg was the place to do it. It took us two overnights to get there. The roads were great, just like driving back in the States. Most of the way was barren rock fields. Among the more notable differences were the baboons sitting alongside the road watching us pass by and the hundreds of ostriches that sat stupidly along the road behind fences. These ridiculous looking birds all curiously watched us approach and then as soon as we got close, the whole herd tried to run down the road to get away from us. I couldn't think of too many sights more hilarious than five hundred terrified ostrich butts jumping up and down in unison.

We arrived in Johannesburg late in the evening and found a cheap hotel, at which point we faced our first technical problem of the journey: Alex's bike wouldn't start back up. For some reason the starter died. We unloaded our gear and sat in the middle of a dark parking lot under a streetlight as we ripped his bike apart. Kris was the first to identify the culprit: a faulty starter relay. We devised a way to bypass the faulty switch in no time, and in less than an hour had the bike running as good as new. We had passed our first test. Our confidence gained momentum.

"Hey, I got an email from Mike," I told the guys when checking messages later on the hotel Internet.

"Does he know when he'll be able to separate from the Air Force?" Kris asked.

"It looks like he'll be joining us around the time we'll be passing through Nairobi."

"Tell him to get a ticket!"

We spent another week in South Africa getting visas before we said good-bye to the last major city we would see until we reached Kenya. We had gotten all of the necessary visas except one. Sudan had approved us for a visa, but hadn't issued it yet and didn't know when they would be able to do so. It could be a day or it could be a month.

"We'll just send the approval to Nairobi," they told us. "When you arrive they will be able to issue the visas there."

"Works for me," I said. We had spent enough time in South Africa. It was time to press on.

The vibration of the engine beneath me, the whistle of the wind whipping past my helmet, I found my place on the highway alongside my friend and brother. We rode in a common solitude, left to our thoughts and wonderings. There was still a lot of road between us and Botswana.

Thank you.

How Fast Can Elephants Run?

Botswana

Kris (left) and Alex making dinner. We always seemed to draw a crowd.

We crossed the border from South Africa into Botswana, the sun hovering just a couple inches over the horizon. The road immediately turned from a well-maintained, four-lane divided highway into a narrow, two-lane strip of weathered asphalt. We could see miles in every direction. The grass was low and dry, but still green, and little scraggy trees poked their heads through here and there. People were scarce; no housing developments were to be seen, only round mud huts with thatched roofs scattered infrequently off the road. This was what I had imagined Africa would look like.

"Where to now?" Kris asked as he looked at a map. I compared it to "Gips," our GPS unit.

"It doesn't look like we're gonna make it to anyplace with a guestroom before dark. Let's keep our eyes open for a place to camp."

We cruised side-by-side, taking up both lanes. We had the road to ourselves. An hour later we saw a filling station. We all agreed to stop.

Behind the gas station we found a very inviting patch of dirt. Not too far away on the other side of a rickety fence dogs were snarling at us. *Good, they'll let us know if any unwelcomed beasts come near our tent.* The old woman who worked the station very kindly agreed to let us sleep there. She even invited us to share her dinner of kudu, a large animal with long twisting antlers that roams the African bush. It was dark now, and we were ready to rest.

The next morning we broke camp early and hit the road. It was another hot day. The unobstructed rays beat down hour after hour. We were sweating under our thick black riding gear, but didn't consider shedding it. We explored Botswana on our motorcycles all day, stopping only twice for simple meals of beans and bread before we finally found a small village. Children ran out to see the three aliens.

"Hello, excuse me!" I shouted.

"Hallo!" answered a man with gray hair carrying a staff.

"My friends and I are looking for a place to rest the night. Could we stay here in your village?"

For a moment he just looked at us, inspecting our strange apparel and the unnatural vehicles that carried us.

"Eh?"

"Sleep, one night," I repeated with accompanying hand signals, finally pointing to a patch of turf just off the road.

"Hallo, yes, okay. Ova here, come, come!" The man started off toward a patch of earth not far away from an old dilapidated one-story structure, lifting his knees high and planting his staff with every step.

The children curiously studied us all evening as we prepared a meal and set up camp. The sun set. We rested. Morning came. We were off again before the children awoke.

Kris and I were riding in front and, after a while, saw a trail made by some large game heading off the road with a couple of basketball-size turds nearby. Kris grinned at me and then shot down the trail; without hesitating I followed close behind. Alex always thought things through a little more thoroughly than

Kris and I and recognized right away that this was probably a bad idea. But what could he do except join us?

Before you think we were too crazy, let me set the stage: Up until this point we had been on boring paved road. We had dirt bikes. We wanted to use them like dirt bikes. Furthermore, we had heard so much about the wildlife in Botswana. People told us that it would be impossible to pass through the country and not see many elephants and giraffes. Yet we had gone two days and not seen anything but hot sun, dry bush, and dusty road. We were ready for a wildlife sighting.

The hot, dusty trail got narrower and narrower until we were just weaving around big piles of poop and scrubby bushes about ten feet tall. We slowed down and stopped next to a large water hole.

Alex caught up. He seemed less than excited about our little excursion. "What in the world are we doing?"

"We're looking for elephants," Kris proudly announced.

"Right, I got that. And if we find an elephant? What then?"

Kris and I exchanged perplexed looks; neither of us really had a plan beyond finding the elephant. That's when it occurred to me: if we were to come upon an elephant right now, we would have no place to go.

"Uh huh," Alex interrupted the silence.

"Oh, well," Kris said. "We're here now."

We shut off the bikes and started looking around. Alex found the tallest tree in sight and spidermanned his way to the top. From there he could see a couple miles in every direction.

"What do you see, bro?"

"Lots of bushes, lots of dry stuff, lots of sun. There are no elephants around here," he announced in a tone that bordered between relieved and disappointed. He came down and we decided to take this opportunity to eat our lavish lunch of sun-warmed refried beans with chili flavoring and a loaf of sliced bread.

I was sprawled out in a patch of shade and Kris and Alex were rummaging through the duffel bag on the back of my bike, when we heard a large branch snap on the other side of the water hole just through a sheet of leaves.

"What's that?"

"Did you guys hear that?"

Snap, another stick crunched. We were straining our eyes, searching the bush at eye level.

Suddenly a massive gray monster emerged—ears spread, eyes fixed on us. I had seen elephants at the zoo and on TV, and they had never struck me as too intimidating of an animal. But when there was no fence or wall to separate the six-plus tons of gray monster from our insignificant, one hundred and sixty-five pounds of pink soft flesh, the elephant took on a whole new image. He was king, and we were at his mercy. We froze. It was clear that the beast had seen us, but we weren't sure yet how he felt about our presence. Alex slowly started to step back. Kris and I grabbed the cameras and started taking pictures.

Then right in front of us the elephant started to take a bath in the nearby water hole. He didn't seem to mind that we were watching him from less than twenty yards away. We watched him for a while, trying to get some good photos, until finally he looked up at us, spread his ears, and charged.

The three of us turned and ran as fast as we could, hoping to lose the beast in the thick bush. All we heard were crashing trees and breaking sticks. I was the first to stop. Not getting trampled by an elephant was right at the top of my to-do list, but not getting separated and lost in the man-eating, animal infested African bush was a none-too-distant second. I listened. I heard splashing. It sounded like he had given up chasing us and returned to his bath.

"Hey, guys!" I yelled while trying to whisper.

"Yo," Kris shouted from a dozen yards away.

"Yeah, is he still chasing us?" Alex was a bit farther off.

"No, he's finishing his bath. What do you say we get out of here?"

We regrouped and got ready to jet. Two of the bikes were about seventy yards away. We got them ready to take off. My bike was much closer and in clear view of the elephant. He was looking right at it. He was probably plotting to come steal our beans and stomp all over our stuff right now.

Kris looked at me. "I've got a plan. Erik, you go jump on your dirt bike and start it up. It's gonna be loud and the elephant will probably charge you again."

"Okay." I was waiting for the rest of the plan.

"I'll have the camera ready. Let him get close, but not so close that you couldn't outrun him."

Alex stared at Kris, amazed.

"Oh, and don't crash either," Kris added.

"Sounds good," I said. Kris reached for his camera and I got ready to run to my bike right next to the conniving pachyderm.

"Whoa, hold on," Alex interjected. "Erik, are you kidding me? You're seriously considering letting that huge monster chase you?"

"Well, yeah, but—"

"Why don't you just sit here for two minutes and wait for the elephant to finish his bath and leave?"

Kris was obviously disappointed, but there was no arguing with Alex's logic.

Sure enough, not thirty seconds later the elephant took one final rinse, looked at us, waved his big gray trunk good-bye, and wandered lazily back into the bush.

Relieved, we quickly hopped on our bikes and got back to the road. It was a short drive to the northern border of Botswana. We saw several more elephants clearly from the road and even a couple of giraffes.

The Zambezi River just upstream from the famous Victoria Falls separated Botswana and Zambia. Here a couple of American dollars would catch you a ride on the ferry across the Zambezi River.

"What's going on over there?" Alex pointed to some commotion on the other side of the river. I squinted my eyes and barely made out a group of men with automatic weapons harassing the people as they got off the ferry.

"Who knows?" It was going to be a couple hours before we boarded the rusty old boat.

CORREN CON LOS TOROS

Southern Zambia

On patrol with paramilitary rangers.

Guards with automatic weapons were waiting for us on the other side of the river. They looked at us suspiciously and then waved us through with the barrels of their weapons. We still needed to get through customs and immigration. I pointed to a relatively secluded corner of the dirt parking lot. Kris was already headed that way.

"Are you guys gonna need any money for this border?" Kris asked as he dug through a duffel for the travel papers.

"A little never hurts," I said. "You ready to do this, Alex?"

"You know it."

I took our passports to the immigrations shack. Alex took our Carnets to the armed customs official. They skeptically examined our paperwork looking for a reason to slap us with some tax or a fine. A little bit of "coffee money" handed clearly over the counter with a smile as a token of appreciation sped the process along.

We rendezvoused back at the bikes. Kris was making sure a curious crowd of opportunists kept their distance from our stuff.

As soon as we crossed the river the terrain transformed from dry bush to lush forest. Victoria Falls was just a short drive away. We saw an old sign advertising 4 x 4 camping a couple kilometers downriver from the falls and shot down a narrow two-track.

"Let's check this place out!" I said. Kris had already started down the trail.

"We could go to any of the campgrounds that we drove by," Alex said. "We don't have to go to the one that may or may not exist who-knows-how-far down this treacherous path, do we?"

"Eh, maybe. Let's check it out."

Alex shook his head, cracked a thin smile, and let out a sigh of acceptance. He would have kept on trying to convince me if I were anyone else. Of course, he was right. This potentially challenging trail was totally unnecessary; we both knew that, but we were at a fork in the road: one paved, one less traveled. I had to see what was at the other end.

I was born to ride dirt bikes. Flying down the rough and narrow trail was amazing. Kris took off ahead, I was second, Alex was close behind. I could hear him cheering. The trail snaked through a small village. I finally knew what quaint looks like: huts with thatched roofs and mud walls, women carrying bundles of firewood on their heads. Everyone loved that we were on motorcycles. They waved and smiled; the children ran out and cheered.

At trail's end we arrived at a beautiful resort, secluded and unique. The central lodge was perched beside a canyon seven hundred feet over the Zambezi River, and a trail led down to the water. The falls were just a couple miles away. We had the whole place nearly to ourselves.

All three of us stood at the edge of the canyon and gazed out at the river below and the country of Zimbabwe on the other side.

We stood silent for a moment. The scene demanded reverence.

"Good call, guys. Nice find," Alex said quietly.

"Yeah, this'll do, " I whispered.

Finances were tight, but today was a day worth celebrating. For the past two weeks we had been eating bread and canned beans almost exclusively—along with whatever food we had been given. We were exhausted and hungry. We decided to treat ourselves to a dinner of hamburgers, grilled chicken, potatoes, roasted onions, and peppers from the local market—all prepared over a jungle fire. I had never been known too well for my cooking abilities, but Alex and Kris were deadly in the kitchen, both born chefs. I couldn't think of a time I had a better meal. We had full stomachs for the first time since South Africa and even had enough left over for breakfast. We set up camp and fell fast asleep.

In the middle of the night I was awakened by some noises near the campfire. *Someone was outside going through our stuff! Wait, there were more than one out there.* Kris had already gotten up to investigate, armed with a knife and a flashlight.

Kris saw it before me and screamed.

Alex and I were out the tent door right behind him in our underwear ready to fight off the would-be bandits.

Right in front of us a gang of monkeys were untying our food and throwing it to their friends in the trees. Kris ran after them, cursing the blasted animals, but it was too late. They had all retreated to the trees, taking our breakfast with them. They perched themselves just out of Kris's reach and laughed at us. A couple of them even had the nerve to throw balls of crumpled up tinfoil and banana peels at him.

Alex and I burst out in laughter. Kris didn't see anything funny about the situation. He was ready to crucify each and every one of those wicked little primates. They just mocked us from the trees until Kris returned to the tent a defeated man.

"Stupid monkeys," was all he could say as he lay back down.

Alex and I laughed until our stomachs hurt. Kris was too infuriated to laugh yet. I went to sleep with a smile on my face, but woke up hungry the next morning.

A few days later, we hiked down the gorge to the rushing Zambezi River, several hundred feet of sheer cliffs on either side. We scampered over big black boulders in our underwear and dove into the cool water—ever watchful for crocs. People on kayaks passed by and looked at us confused. I could just about hear them thinking, How in the world did these guys get here?

Any excuse at all would get us on our bikes and down the trail. Just riding that trail through the forest was reason enough. We were getting more and more confident on our stallions. We spent the nights talking around a campfire, discussing hopes and dreams, about how life was meant to be lived. I was content. I missed nothing and wanted nothing. All that I needed was right there with me: each other and a task. We were seeing and experiencing a part of life that so few realize. I had no doubt in my mind: this trip with these men was right where I was supposed to be. The whisper was silent.

✦

"Did you guys really run with the bulls in Pamplona?" Kris asked one night as the campfire embers glowed and the river and jungle competed for most background noise.

"Yep," Alex said.

"What was that like?"

"It's a long story."

"You got somewhere else to be?"

I laughed. "Alex was still living in southern Spain and I was in Al Hoceima helping out with the earthquake relief project. I managed to finagle a three-day weekend the week of the running of the bulls. I caught the overnight ferry traveling across the Mediterranean to Spain, crawled into a corner of the boat, and fell asleep for the entire eight hours of the trip. The low drone of the engines put me right to sleep."

Alex sat up. "I still had classes in Malaga. Erik called the night before so I knew he made it onto the Thursday night ferry. Halfway through one of my classes, he shows up at my school with his backpack, ready to go."

"Right. Alex tells me to go down to the beach and chill for another hour while he goes to his last class. Then it hits me that I had no idea how we were going to get to Pamplona. It was completely on the other side of the country, near the French border. Even if we were able to get there, we had no accommodations. We didn't know anyone up there we could stay with, we didn't have any reservations, and we knew all the hostels would be full. Even if we could find a room, we didn't have any money. When I had last visited Alex a week earlier, I asked if he could figure it all out, but it was not until that moment as I sat on the beach in the shade waiting for him to get out of class that I realized how big of a challenge that would be— "

"Erik, I told you I'd take care of it."

"I know, and I hadn't so much as given it a thought since I had left, but I began to wonder. How could you have figured it out? I wouldn't know where to start, and I had been in Spain for a year and knew the language. You were eighteen years old, alone in a foreign country, speaking a foreign language, and had only been there a couple weeks.

"I looked at my watch. The hour was up so I made my way back to the school. It was noon. As I got closer I saw Alex running my direction."

"Poor Erik had no idea what was going on when I started yelling at him. 'Got everything you need? 'Cause we gotta go!' The bus that ran to the center of town was approaching us from behind. We had to run to beat it to the stop."

"At this point I am thoroughly lost, when Alex starts filling me in on the plan: he has a rental car waiting for us. Then he asks, 'You've got your ID, right?' He was too young to rent or drive the rental car, but he reserved one for us."

"Hold on a second," Kris stopped us. "How did you know where to reserve a rental car, Alex?"

"I just went to the airport. I figured a lot of people who didn't know Spanish but needed cars went through there every day. It was a piece of cake."

"Not bad," Kris answered, looking at me obviously impressed.

"I know," I responded. "We hopped on the bus and found our seats while Alex explained the plan to me. We go, rent the car, make the alleged twelve-hour drive up to Pamplona. We sleep in the car for as long as we stay, run with the bulls, party like maniacs, then drive back. He had class on Monday and I had to be back to work in Morocco. It was going to be quick and dirty, and we didn't have a plan other than where we were going. The car was waiting for us at the airport. Eight and a half hours later we were pulling into Pamplona, Spain. Alex knew we could drive it faster than the normal twelve hours."

"Kris," Alex started, "I have never seen another party like that in all my life. Have you, Erik?"

"No way."

He continued: "The whole city dressed up in red and white, parading in the streets. They said that some three and a half million people jam into Pamplona to experience one of the biggest parties known to man. Erik and I didn't waste any time. We explored the city, scouted out the course we would be running the following morning, and bought matching white outfits with red sashes to put round our necks and waists. That night we found an old factory parking lot to sleep in."

"What's scarier than a three quarter-ton beast with spears on his head trying to bore through you?" I asked Kris.

He promptly replied, "A six-and-a-half-ton beast with a snake for a nose trying to stomp you to death."

"Touché," chirped Alex.

For a second I forgot my company, thinking about how six of these massive bulls chased us down a tight street with nowhere to go but through us. "Yeah, that was pretty scary now that you mention it."

Alex took over: "We got up early, dressed in our new clothes, and went to the street to pick our spot. The cops soon came through and kicked everyone out of the street. Apparently we were supposed to go through a specific entrance to run. Erik starts yelling for me to follow him and takes off through the crowd."

"I ran under a barrier back along the street. We found a section of barrier where the runners were awaiting the bulls. It was patrolled by two policemen," I added.

"I'm doing my best to keep up with Erik and then all of a sudden he says, 'Wait. Wait. GO!' I was still trying to figure out what he was talking about when he takes off through the barricade just as the two cops turn their backs to us. I was right behind him when the cops hear us, turn around, and start yelling. They were never going to find us in that maze of red and white. We disappeared."

I interrupted. "We were on the route with the rest of the runners. They let us get our head start before releasing the bloodthirsty bulls. Alex and I went to the infamous ninety-degree corner. We stopped in the middle of the road and waited."

"Waited?" Kris chimed in inquisitively.

"Yeah, we were waiting for the bulls, baby," Alex answered with big eyes as he relived the moment.

"I told Alex that when the bulls came, to run as fast as he could. Don't look back, just run. Over people, around people, whatever, just run. I would be right behind him. The first flare went off and the bulls were in the street. People panicked and began running by us."

"They ran by us, but we didn't move," Alex explained. "The first crowd passed and another crowd came. The faces in the second crowd were white, with a look of terror written across them. They had seen the bulls. Sure enough, the bulls were no more than seventy yards out, smashing people as they made their way up the street. And that's when I got my butt out of there pronto."

"We got halfway up the street before Alex looked back. I was right behind him, but he didn't even see me. His mouth dropped open, his eyes got huge, and he cut a ninety-degree turn, running full speed to the wall. *I bet I'm about to get gored* was all I could think as I looked over my shoulder."

"When I looked back, Erik was just a couple feet behind me, but a couple more feet behind him was the first of six huge man cows ready to run through all of us. I was getting out of Erik's way. He was about to get hit!"

Kris was laughing almost uncontrollably at the scene, which I never had thought too comical before that day.

"There was already a group stuck to the wall where Alex had found refuge. I would be on the outside unless I kept running. Up ahead there was a doorway. I cut out in front of the bulls, around the crowd, and into the doorjamb. The six massive monsters ran by just barely grazing the crowd as they passed. For the moment the tension eased. I found Alex; we were both so high on our own adrenaline we were euphoric: We were still alive."

"Then people began shouting and yelling again," Alex said. "More bulls were coming. Erik and I ran together as fast as our legs would carry us another quarter mile up to the bullring. We got into the ring and congratulated ourselves on a job well done. Just then a herd of steers ran through the crowd into the ring and then out the tunnel at the other end of the arena. There we were, all three hundred of us who had made it into the ring thus far. They closed the doors, locking us in. The crowd was cheering; we, the victors, looked at each other with an awesome sense that we are now among the elite few to have conquered the famous running of the bulls. We had made it."

"Or so we thought," I interjected.

"The crowd split. On the other side of the arena people were being tossed into the air. Erik and I had no idea what was going on. Then it hit us. They let a bull free into the crowd!"

"Yeah, they sure did. The crowd of spectators wasn't cheering for us, they were cheering for the bulls brutalizing us. This cracked-out bull was charging everyone. It ran right by me and I smacked it on the butt as it passed by. Alex, not to be outdone, sought out the bull and gave it his own smack."

"Naturally," Kris added.

"Oh yeah, I hit that bull hard enough to stop him in his tracks. He turned around, looked directly at me, and charged."

"So guess what he does?" I asked. "Let me preface this by saying that when they start charging, bulls don't stop until they either hit you or something else gets in their way."

Kris started laughing again, already knowing where this was going.

"He ran as fast as he could directly into the center of the group watching nearby and ducked behind some other guy. The bull hardly noticed the switch as he plowed into the crowd. Alex got away scot-free with quite a story."

Kris was now physically in pain as he was laughing so hard, imagining the scene.

"What? They shouldn't have gotten so close to the bull if they didn't want to get hit," Alex announced in a vain attempt to justify the move.

"They let six more bulls out into the crowd after we thought it was over. All in all, the experience lasted about an hour. One hour of heart-pounding thrills. It was a good day."

"So good we had to do it again the next morning," said Alex.

"After the run we stumbled back to the car dirty and tired, adrenaline still pumping through our veins. We drove down the road looking for a place to wash up before we passed out in a field somewhere.

"That night we partook in the festivities. We were heroes. We had run with the bulls and survived. Everyone wanted to hear our stories. Alex and I danced the night away with the rest of the city. And the next morning, after just three hours of sleep, we ran again."

"Ahhhh," Alex let out a sigh.

It was dark; we were all tired.

"Not bad, guys," Kris concluded. "Sounds like Mike and I need to find our way over to Pamplona."

"You'll love it," Alex said. "I can't wait to take my kids."

We all three chuckled, but he was serious.

"Let's get some sleep," I said. "Tomorrow's gonna be a long day."

"How many hours is it to our next stop?"

"If all goes as planned, maybe four."

But in Africa things never go as planned.

Kris (left) and I before a quick dip.

DEEP INTO THE GREEN

Zambia

The road to Lusaka was for the most part paved. It was just one day's travel north to the city. The air carried three distinct scents: diesel fuel, campfire, fresh flowers — or some combination thereof. The land was green with tall hills rising up on the sides of the road. The land that wasn't forest was covered by six-foot-tall grass, so thick that you couldn't see more than a foot into it. Most of the mornings started off sunny, clouds usually formed in the afternoon, and showers seemed to be an inevitable part of early evening.

Lusaka was a dirty city full of crowded streets, pushy merchants, and desperate beggars. We didn't spend long there before pressing further north to pass the night.

We were in no huge rush, as our next contact meeting wasn't for two weeks and several hundred miles to the north in Burundi. So whenever we saw a possible point of interest, we checked it out. It usually turned out to be nothing, but a couple of times we got lucky.

Once I saw a small sign with faded letters that read: "Waterfall, 20 km." Without letting off the throttle, we exchanged gestures. Alex and I wanted to take the detour. Kris was anxious to carry on. We decided to check it out.

The trail took us deeper into the green, right to a dazzling waterfall fed by a cool but powerful stream and ending in a thunderous pool — and we had this Never Never Land all to ourselves. I was looking for fairies flying through the trees. We stripped down and dove into the cool refreshing pool with a bar of soap. It had been days since we last bathed and it could get dreadfully hot underneath our riding jackets.

Alex was still swimming while Kris and I lay on a rock in the sun.

"Have you ever seen anything so spectacular?" I asked.

"This is it, brother," Kris responded.

Thank you.

He turned his head and looked at me.

"So what happened in Morocco, Erik?"

"A lot happened, what are you talking about?"

"When you left Colorado you seemed so restless and discontent. Now you seem to have found whatever it was you were looking for. What happened to you over there?"

Alex was kicking like a frog closer to the falls.

It didn't look like he was coming back anytime soon. And I was ready to talk.

"By the fall after I got to Melilla, all of the summer projects had finished up. The groups of churchgoers slowed down until finally the last group, a bunch from Northern Ireland, handed out their last package and went home. The distribution had ended altogether and for the first time since I had landed, there was peace and quiet in Melilla. It would be a couple months before any new projects started. Some of the team had to go back to the UK for a while on business so there was little to be done in Melilla. However, the time was not to be wasted.

"Paul asked Diego and me to spend the next three months in Morocco in the ancient city of Fez, familiarizing ourselves with Moroccan culture and studying the official language of Morocco: Arabic. Obviously, we were both thrilled about the opportunity. Fez was one of the oldest medieval cities in the world, second only to the Khan al-Khalili market in Cairo. It was home to the oldest university in the world, a source of legend and mystery for centuries. In its long and eventful history, Fez had become familiar with very few white people. Soon I would be added to the list. It appeared that Diego and I would be spending a lot of time together over the next year or so.

"Ever since the day when Diego and I were jammed into the sweltering backseat of Paul's minivan we had an unspoken understanding. We were sitting there miserably hot, counting the seconds until we could escape the torture of being forced to listen to a group of churchgoers sing 'Kumbaya.' It was awful. Diego had the foresight to bring a DiskMan with a ready supply of heavy metal and was benevolent enough to let me have an earbud. We naturally became good friends after that. Every couple of days he and I would go out after the church groups had gone to sleep for the night and talk over a beer.

"Diego was the only person on the team who I felt I could really connect with. Everyone else seemed to be so far above my struggles but he, like me, was a work in progress with a long way to go. And to him it seemed to matter less where we were on the journey and more what direction we were going. He was not ignorant to the darker side of this life, having been adopted from a life of drug addiction and gangs in Argentina at the age of sixteen, and as a result was able to embrace love and grace in a way that few could.

"In our late-night talks, I confided in him my worries, regrets, hopes, and fears. I told him how concerned I was that the rest of the team would find out that I had never been to church camp, that I didn't know the words to any of the hymns they sang. Kris, you know how much trouble we got into growing up. No one else on the team knew what the back of a cop car looked like. The people we grew up with were not all good kids from happy families. Many are either in jail, burned out on drugs, or dead. This world that the rest of the team seemed to live in was something altogether foreign to me. But Diego had had it as rough as anyone and here he was. He had made plenty of his own mistakes and had his own worries and concerns, his own doubts and questions, but he was striving toward an ideal.

"He, like I, believed that there was a good and a right way to live and that one's obligation was to pursue that path. There were constants. Right and wrong were not relative, but each person's journey varied. We both believed that the same higher power that had stitched us together in our mothers' wombs had instilled a sense of justice and right and wrong, and it was that same power that had led us to Morocco and introduced us to one another.

"While it did seem a little far-fetched even to me, I truly believed that we could reach out to this power. I suppose the very fact that I had such a longing could be construed as evidence that there was a listening ear on the other end of my prayers. Where else would that desire come from if not from that which created me? I reached out to this power and asked for guidance."

Kris nodded his head, urging me to continue.

"I was still searching, yet I already knew what I would discover. I had sought truth and this was where I ended up. I had been surrounded by these good men and women, all ardent believers in Christianity. If there was a higher power working to reveal the truth, then it was no coincidence that I had landed in Melilla and been surrounded by all these people of genuine faith.

"The days passed quickly, our talks filled the nights. Before I knew it, the time had come to travel to Fez. We braved the chaos of the Melilla/Morocco border. The space in between the Moroccan and Spanish border, no man's land as it was called, was utter pandemonium that morning. Hundreds of men and women scurried around with their illegally smuggled goods. Corrupt Moroccan officers chased the masses with cruel rubber hoses, slashing blindly into the crowds. This was not an uncommon scene; however, it was the first time we were crossing the border without Paul and the safety of the van. It was at this border that I had personally witnessed a man smuggle a full-size refrigerator into Morocco on the back of a beat-up old bicycle. Diego and I didn't know what to make of the scene, but that was the only way into Morocco. We walked straight through the crowd with our backpacks on, passports tightly in hand. The guards seemed to pay no attention to us as we passed through the checkpoints. From the other side of the border, it cost only 50 dirham ($5) for a tight seat in an old taxi. It was a full day's travel to Fez.

"We arrived late in the afternoon. Paul had made arrangements for us to live with a Moroccan family in one of the oldest corners of the city. For the next several weeks we would be sleeping on a hard tile floor and bathing on the roof in a room full of live sheep with a bucket of cold water. This was our new home.

"The three months that Diego and I spent in Fez were exhausting, but time passed quickly. Coming back to Melilla was a welcomed relief. It was like stepping back inside a heated home on a cold winter day. The language was so much more welcoming, the Spanish culture felt so comfortable and familiar. It was around this time that I had my first encounter with the refugees.

"The team was back together and I didn't feel nearly as distanced from them as I did when I had first arrived just months prior. I think it was because I had seen and felt in my own life some of the things that I saw them living out. I had prayed and seen prayers answered. I had called out to God and felt in my heart that he really heard me. I believed and my faith was growing stronger every day. I still thought some of the things the team did were kind of weird. I was very different than they were, but I had begun to realize that those differences did not make me less able to live for God. So I didn't like evening sing-a-longs, and I thought most of the board games they played were dumb. I still liked MTV. I liked beer. That didn't mean that I couldn't live for God. Living for God wasn't about creating a huge list of things I didn't do. And it wasn't about being a 'good boy.' It was about realizing what I was created to do and being courageous enough to embrace it. Paul and his team were all awesome people, each worthy of every respect, but even they were travelers on the road, just like me, just like Diego. They were living as best they knew how, but they hadn't arrived at the 'right life' yet either. No one ever arrives; we are always exploring and discovering and aspiring. For the first time in my life, I felt good about where I was going.

"What's more, Diego and I managed to land a pretty nice place. It was far more than we had hoped for, but I was learning that when you follow the voice inside the whole universe works together to help you in your travels. It was a very simple home in a squatter village. There were three bedrooms, three bathrooms, and a full-size kitchen. By far the most impressive feature of our new home was that it sat on the top of a hill, just a stone's throw away from two-hundred-foot cliffs and the Mediterranean below. I have always loved the sea and loved to rock climb, and there wasn't a better house in all of Melilla for me.

"After we moved in, I would climb down to the sea every day with my rock climbing shoes and a bag of chalk and boulder along the cliffs over the sea. It was a great way to start the day, and it was here that I found I had my best times with God."

Kris looked at me with one eyebrow raised.

"I know, Kris, it always bothers me when people say they had a talk with God, or God told them to do this or that. I once heard an overzealous messenger of the Word say that God tapped him on the shoulder and jerked him from his unfulfilling career, as if God appeared to these people and spoke his will for their lives with unmistakable clarity. I have seen such talk be used to justify some very questionable behavior and some of the most illogical decisions as a sort of, 'It's not my fault, God told me to do it.'"

Kris nodded his head in affirmation.

"First of all," I continued, "I think that those people who describe their relationship with their creator like this are almost always full of it. Second, I think that kind of talk propagates the notion that people like me who don't get messages directly from the heavens are less able to communicate with our creator. I want to be very clear. God has never spoken to me in an audible voice, no angel has ever come to me in a dream, I am no prophet, but I do believe that we are able to communicate on an incomprehensible level with the power that created us. When I say I had my best times with God when I was down at the beach, hanging off a cliff, the surf crashing below me, I am referring to a deep inner peace, an awareness that at that moment I was intimately connected with something so right and good and pure that it had to be God."

Kris looked around him, still trying to take in the beauty of our surroundings, and with another deep breath said, "I feel ya, E. I'm proud of you."

Alex swam through the current up to the side of the pool. "That felt good. What do ya think? You guys about ready to hit the road again?"

"Yeah," I said. "It's probably about that time, huh?"

Kris grabbed his backpack. I tossed Alex his pants.

We took one last look at the falls. We were clean. We were refreshed. We were ready to travel.

"It's been a long road, huh Erik?" Kris said.

"We're going the right way," I answered.

We had two more hours of uneventful road before we got to the next town. There we met a man who apparently had some responsibility over Zambia's big game reserves. The parks were not open to tourism during this time of year, but I think he mistook us for important people and arranged for a visit deep into the parks. The next closest fueling station was 500 km to the north in Tanzania, so we each carried jerry cans with ten extra liters of petrol. It was 60 km of tarmac road to the turnoff, then another 80 km of sand and mud to our destination. It was tough going.

Twenty kilometers into the trail, Kris lost control and crashed. One of his jerry cans burst open, spilling fuel all over him and the hot engine and exhaust. Kris was calm. He tried to free himself from under his bike, but his leg was pinned. The fuel soaked through his clothes and covered his skin. Our eyes locked. I needed to get there now. Kris was silent. He knew I was coming and that was enough. He just waited and hoped to God that fuel didn't spark.

Please don't light. Please don't let that fuel spark.

I jumped off my bike and started trying to lift his bike off him. Between the sand and the way he was positioned, I couldn't even budge it.

"ALEX!"

"I'm here. LIFT!" Alex lifted from the back cargo rack. I heaved again on the handlebars. The bike lifted and Kris scampered out from the fire-hot block of steel.

He got away from the bike. If it burst into flames Alex and I could run.

We stood the bike up.

"Thanks, guys," Kris said casually. "That was a close one, huh?"

Alex and I just looked at each other. If that gas had sparked, there would have been no putting Kris out.

Twenty-five kilometers deeper into the jungle and we arrived at the park headquarters. I noticed on the logbook we signed that we were the tenth group to go beyond this gate so far this year. All of the other entries were official business.

The next stretch of trail was even worse, but our numerous crashes were never too bad. We crossed several rivers using wooden bridges built from the nearby trees. Sometimes there was no bridge at all, and we just gunned it through the streams. We turned a bend in the road. One such stream was just ahead. It looked deep and the water was moving fast. Alex was in the lead. He stopped just short. Kris and I stopped a bit further back.

"What do you think, Erik? I bet we could make it."

"There's no other road. Besides, it's a bit warm; we could use a quick dip."

Alex opened his throttle and plowed his way through the river, sending a wedge of water flying away from his bike. As long as we could keep water out of the air intake, these bikes would keep running. I heard a shout over the splashing.

"YEEHAW."

Oh, that's my brother.

"You ready, K?"

"You know it."

He was second through the water. Alex was victoriously awaiting him, drenched on the other side, ready to coach him through.

"Watch out over here! There's a couple boulders under the water."

Kris was through. It was my turn. *God, I love this stuff: crazy, brutal, perfect.*

After four hours of this abuse, we arrived at a wildlife scout camp where about twenty people lived, eight of whom were paramilitary officers responsible for tracking and capturing poachers. It truly was a wild place. After the sun set I could hear elephants running through the fields, I could hear the hippos in the river about five hundred meters from where we were. Thunderstorms lit the night sky in the distance, but overhead shone countless stars, reflections of the hidden treasures yet to be discovered on this vast and mysterious continent.

The men in the camp were warm and welcoming. There were more than seventy different tribes in Zambia, each with its own dialect, but lucky for us, when the colonial powers arbitrarily drew Zambia's borders on a map and the English moved in, they also decided that English would be Zambia's official language. The men invited us to their fire to roast some peanuts they had harvested earlier that day. After dark, no one dared to venture outside of the camp; to do so was to become a snack for some beast hiding in the trees. We spent most of the evening answering each others' questions about our homes, Africa and America. They asked me in utter disbelief if it was really true that every person in America has a personal car and that in America there are markets that never close and have every type of food you can imagine. I was embarrassed to tell them yes.

It was my turn. "Is it true that most people in Zambia don't ever see the age of forty?"

"Oh yeah, forty is very, very old man in Zambia."

I caught Alex's eye, and he was looking at me with a smirk on his face.

"What's on your mind?"

"You don't know?"

"I don't know what?"

"Hey, big brother. Happy twenty-second birthday."

Wow, was it my birthday? I had stopped trying to keep track of the days long before, but I looked at my watch, and, sure enough, it was just after midnight early on February 17.

Kris just laughed.

"Thanks, Alex."

He reached out his hand and gave me my birthday present: a couple of roasted peanuts. "We'll celebrate both of ours together over a steak and a tall beer when we get back to Michigan," he promised.

"Sounds good to me, bro." I couldn't think of any better gift than to be right where I was at that moment with the people I most loved, sharing the adventure of a lifetime.

We stayed at the camp for two days before we returned to the tarmac road and pressed on to Tanzania.

One of a million roadside repairs.

THE NEW DRIVER
Zambia

Heading north out of Zambia the road got progressively worse. It started with a pothole here and there. Then the potholes got bigger, the paved sections smaller until the road was more potholes than asphalt. The bumps shot through the bikes and straight up our backs. We had to stand up so our knees could absorb the brunt of the uneven terrain. The sun was beating down, but my underwear and socks were still soaked from the thunderstorm we drove through not an hour earlier. The pavement stopped altogether now and the road was nothing more than a worn strip of dusty earth around green, tree-covered hills accented by an occasional patch of gray rock jutting from the seamless ground.

Until this point paved road had connected all the places we needed to go. We had spent some time on dirt roads, but it had always been an excursion that we could have avoided. Kris and I were the most excited; for the first time we were being forced to use our dirt bikes as dirt bikes. We went tearing down the road, sending mud splattering over our facemasks and windscreens.

Children heard us coming and ran out of their huts up to the road, where they waited in anticipation for us to pass. The kids seemed to do one of two things. One group crouched down ready to sprint; as soon as we drew near they took off and raced us in their bare feet. Not winning the race didn't discourage them from celebrating. Time and time again the view in our mirrors was of children jumping and cheering us on. The other group seemed to me a little less conventional: these children hurried to the side of the road as we approached, but ran terrified back to their huts as soon as the first bike passed. When all seemed safe, they turned around again and ran back to the road—just in time to catch the second bike drive by. The same thing happened, and inevitably the person riding in back would see the same kids run to and away from the road as he drove by.

It was about four in the afternoon when we reached the border between Zambia and Tanzania. From the map, it looked like a pretty popular border crossing, with a major roadway and city just on the other side. If all went well, we would be able to fill up on gas and withdraw some local currency.

Instead of the official customs station with anal-retentive border officials to which we had become accustomed, we found a group of one-room white homes. Chickens and goats wandered at liberty and a small unkempt gate—the kind that farmers back in the States used to keep their cows from wandering out of the pastures—stretched just barely across the road. This was the border, the official divide between two nations—nothing more than a raggedy old gate with not so much as a fence on either side.

We waited for an official to direct us, but we didn't see any instructions or anything we recognized as a government building. Finally I asked a man walking through the border unchecked, "Where is the customs officer? We need our traveling documents filled out."

"Oh yeah, he live ova da," he said pointing to one of the small homes.

We rode up to the front door and were about to knock when a man groggily came stumbling out, tucking in his shirt. Not trying to hide his annoyance, he informed us that we had woken him in the middle of his nap.

"Um, we're sorry. Just passin' through."

He seemed satisfied. Together we went to another small building and watched him lazily fill out our Carnet du Passage and certify it with an official stamp.

"Da you go." He pointed northeast to Tanzania and motioned for us to leave.

"What about our passports and visas?" Alex asked.

"Oh, you need da immigration offica. He not here now; he been gone three days. Maybe tomorrow he come back? He in the village you come tru; you go find him if you want stamps."

The sun was sinking and the road to Tanzania was feeling more and more remote.

"Let's just get out of here," Kris suggested.

Alex and I quickly agreed. We fired up our bikes and shot around the gate. As we were driving away I looked over my shoulder to see if anyone was concerned that we had just left Zambia without any of the proper stamps. Their only customs officer was wandering back to his home to resume his nap.

Down a footpath over a small stream, a few men were walking casually between the two countries. Less than a mile later we reached the Tanzanian border. Again, no one seemed the least bit concerned about our presence as we parked and walked up to the only shack around. No one was there and the doors were locked. We couldn't enter the country without buying a visa, and we needed our Carnets du Passage filled out; without the necessary paperwork we'd be arrested when we tried to leave the country. We just stood there trying to decide our next move.

A few moments passed before a group of men wearing no distinguishing badges or uniforms finished up a conversation they were having a hundred feet away and wandered over to the border station. Usually Kris stayed with the bikes while Alex and I went in to get the appropriate documents filled out and pay the officials, but at this particular stop there seemed to be little need to guard the bikes. A couple of chickens were the extent of the traffic, clucking in the dusty road as they went about their business of finding bugs.

Alex took our passports and Carnets into the shack to talk to the officials. Kris and I reclined comfortably in the shade of a full green tree.

A few minutes later, Alex joined us.

"They're looking at our stuff. It's gonna be a while."

Kris leaned over his elbow, "I'm sure you got it handled."

"The kid knows how to take care of business," I agreed.

"Sounds like a story."

"Of course."

+

"Back in Al Hoceima, we were swamped, clearing future building sites in the villages in addition to several other projects. All summer Alex had directed the volunteer help that came through the house. He was responsible for assigning different teams to different sites, transporting everyone, supplying tools, teaching new help how the job was done—the works. On top of that he labored like a dog, digging alongside the volunteers.

"When fall came, all the volunteer teams stopped coming. It was just us and our Moroccan friends at the house. I was busy trying to negotiate some of the other projects, but we still needed someone to direct the government-assigned front-end loader drivers. So I asked Alex to fill in for me. One day we got a new driver, and it was his first time behind the wheel. I was in town meeting with a couple other NGOs, when I got a call from Alex. All he said was, 'Erik, this new driver sucks. He's gonna get somebody killed. What should I do?' I was busy and couldn't really talk with him about the situation then, and I certainly couldn't drive out to the job site any time in the next couple hours.

"I responded with only, 'I don't know, Alex. You're in charge. Do what you have to do, okay?'

"As soon as the meetings ended, I called Alex. He didn't pick up. I started getting nervous. First chance I got, about three hours after his concerned call, I shot out to the work site. I could see the dust in the air up on the hillside as soon as I pulled into the valley of Ait Dowd. I could tell they had moved a lot that day. They must have finished at least a few sites while I was in town. As I nosed up the narrow dusty two-track through the massive six-foot-high groves of prickly pears toward the fallen houses, I could see a large crowd of villagers had gathered and were watching our front-end loader labor away. I parked the truck and got out, still looking for Alex. I could see Muhumid. He was on the ground helping direct the front-end loader like always. There was little Mo standing faithfully, waiting for a job he could help with and there was the ... no ... there was the government-appointed driver sitting at the edge of the crowd watching. I looked closely at the guy in the driver's seat wearing a baseball cap and sunglasses — my brother."

Kris was looking at Alex, once again duly impressed.

"I ran up to the site. He didn't even see me at first. He just kept moving the rubble and leveling the ground, eyes fixed on Muhumid for signals. 'Keep going, too far, good.' I couldn't believe it. We had played around in the front-end loader a little bit in the evenings when we weren't working, but actually accomplishing precision work? *Where in the world did he learn how to do this?* Just then one of the villagers came up to me and said in Arabic, 'Your brother's good. He works like champ!'

"Finally Alex saw me. He lowered the scoop and climbed out. Muhumid ran up to me first to explain the situation, not knowing how I would react to my eighteen-year-old brother firing the forty-five-year-old driver that the government had assigned us. They would be irate if anything had happened to their machine while Alex was behind the wheel, but Muhumid assured me that Alex had made a good decision. Then Alex walked up and patted Muhumid on the shoulder and in perfect Arabic said, 'Thanks, my friend. Good work today.' Then he looked at me and cracked a half smile. 'You said I was in charge and this is what needed to happen.' I was shocked and I asked him when he learned how to drive a front-end loader and speak Arabic. He just laughed and said he'd tell me on the way home, as he hopped in the shotgun seat of the truck.

"The villagers all waved and thanked us for the day's work as the team loaded into the truck. 'We'll see you tomorrow,' was the last thing I heard them say. Alex, you looked back, remember? Did you understand that they were expecting you back the next day?"

"Oh sure. They made a point of telling me that long before you picked us up."

I turned back to Kris. "What Alex won't tell you is that they were working on the side of a ridge and the uneven ground made it very difficult to negotiate that fifteen-ton hunk of steel."

"Yeah, at one point that morning the driver rocked two wheels off the ground," Alex said. "The tractor was about to tip over but then somehow it righted itself again. I just watched, praying that this guy didn't get anybody hurt. Less than ten minutes later, the same thing happened again. All the villagers were gathered around nervously watching, waiting for the next mistake. That's when I called Erik. I knew this guy couldn't work that day. I knew if I didn't do something, the equipment was going to get damaged and people might get hurt. What I didn't know is whether or not it was my place to tell a 'qualified' man over twice my age that he was done. If Erik had told him he was fired, that would have been okay—he was the one who paid their checks. But I wasn't sure how much say I had. When I got off the phone with Erik, I knew what I had to do. And get this: when I relieved the driver from his position, he actually thanked me."

"Right, booting the government driver was a good decision, gutsy but necessary. But what impressed me the most was that Alex stepped right up to take his place on a challenging site with a whole crowd skeptically watching and thousands of dollars on the line," I continued. "But even though Alex had only been around the front-end loader for the past couple weeks, he had seen it operate and even spent a little time behind the wheel on easier sites. He was confident that he knew how this site should be done. He knew at what angles the tractor should approach the load. He knew how steep of grade the tractor could safely drive over. Besides, he said that driving the front-end loader was just like playing a video game, and he got a feel for the controls in no time."

"Why wouldn't I have done it?" Alex asked Kris and me.

"Just because people know they can do something doesn't mean they'll have the confidence to do it when there's so much on the line," Kris explained to Alex. "You should be proud of yourself. Just curious: do you have a hard time finding underwear that fits?"

I about lost it, and Alex smirked.

"That doesn't explain his sudden ability to communicate!" I said.

"Yeah, what about that?" Kris asked.

"Alex had been spending most workdays with Muhumid and Arabic was always spoken in the house. Though his exposure to the language was relatively brief, it had been enough for them to develop some basic communication. Alex was picking up some Arabic but most of their communicating was just a game of charades. Muhumid had seen Alex drive the tractor before, and he drove the truck all the time. So I guess they thought it was only natural that Alex climbed in and became the operator, while Muhumid became his eyes. The hand signals they had been using for a couple weeks worked just as well through the windshield as they did standing next to each other.

"In the car on the way home I asked Alex if he wanted to keep driving until the government sent another official driver."

"Like he really needed to ask," Alex chimed in.

"For the next week and a half, Alex was the full-time driver. Muhumid decided where they would work and how much they would do and constantly communicated with Alex via their ever-evolving signal language. Whenever arguments started about whether or not we could do extra work for the villagers, Muhumid would say, 'Sorry it's the boss's call,' and point to Alex, who would give a completely ignorant nod affirming whatever Muhumid had decided. They were a perfect team—so perfect that Alex even managed to clear and level a site that the former driver refused to do because it was too challenging.

"The time flew by and before we knew it, they found a replacement driver. Alex went back to helping Muhumid with decisions and whatnot. When I went to pick them up at the end of the day, the villagers made it very clear that they didn't like Alex's replacement. They wanted Alex back working in their village!" I said, giving him a slap on the shoulder. "Muhumid just laughed as the homeowners told me that Alex worked harder and better than this new guy. I asked them to give it a couple of days and we would see. But you must have done something right, since they all wanted you back."

Alex just grinned.

"Two days later they hadn't changed their minds, and the driver was more than willing to step down. He was a hundred percent Arab and hadn't reconciled the cultural differences. He had worked for the Riffis long enough. For the rest of the time Alex was the full-time driver."

"Not bad, bro," Kris said. Alex was just sitting silently in the shade, a little bit embarrassed that I had bragged him up so much.

"It wasn't half as big of a deal as Erik makes it sound."

Kris smiled, looking at one of the chickens that had just found a bug and was clucking happily. The air was cool and the sun was bouncing off the trees sideways, making the blue sky and the green land come alive. No one else came or went in the hour it took the border officials to finish our paperwork. The sun was setting. It would be less than an hour before we lost the light altogether, and we still had no idea where we were going to stay the night.

We mounted our stallions. They each let out a roar as we headed down the road.

Alex is taking the picture. As always, village children flocked to him.

CHARADES

Southwestern Tanzania

The town we were expecting turned out to be yet another invention of a mapmaker. The major roadway that we thought would take us through this country proved to be nothing more than a narrow dirt path in very poor condition.

"The log at the border station showed that we're the first vehicles to travel this road in twelve days," Alex announced. "It doesn't look like we'll be able to get any gas or change any money here."

Kris and I both laughed.

"Let's keep our eyes open for a place to camp," I said.

Green hills surrounded us as far as we could see in any direction. One narrow brown strip cut through the valley to mark our path. Down the path we rode. Eventually we came upon the first group of huts.

"Let's see if we can stay here."

A boy stepped out of a hut along the road and stared at us, motionless.

"Hi, there. Do you know of a place we can camp for the night?"

He just returned a blank and intimidated stare. His father came outside and said something to us in Swahili. Up until now English had been the national language or at least widely spoken in the countries we were traveling through. Now a language barrier offered yet another challenge to our travels.

We began a game of charades. I was the primary mime; Alex and Kris filled in the blanks. Like actors in a silent film the three of us put on a collaborative effort trying to convey to this man that we wanted to sleep in his field. I can only imagine what he must have been thinking of us: three white men ride from the middle of nowhere on a road that maybe saw traffic semi-weekly, wearing what must have looked to him like alien apparel—silver helmets with a clear facemask, heavy-duty jackets, and pants in a place where the temperature rarely drops below seventy-five. I'm surprised the very sight of us didn't scare him away! Then to add to the awkwardness we start dancing around these bi-wheeled contraptions like three mutes.

Whatever was going through this man's mind I will never know. He uttered just one word, "NO," and pointed further down the road.

"Well, that was smooth," I said with a laugh.

"Eh, I thought you were a very convincing mime," Alex reassured me.

That's my brother, always there to put a positive spin on things.

The next group of huts we came across was more impressive—probably one hundred in all. Children again ran to the road to witness the loud rumble approaching their village. We slowed down and stood up on our foot pegs to better survey the village, looking for someone we could speak with. We must have looked like marauders to these kids, who were dressed in filthy rags. Only a fortunate few had both pants and shirt; the majority ran shamelessly with exposed bottoms. They looked destitute, skinny, and malnourished; several had swollen pot bellies from the parasites living inside of them. We stopped and again tried to communicate through our now well rehearsed games of charades that we were looking for a place to spend the night. This village was much more receptive than the other. They motioned for us to stay and some children ran off into the village.

"Do you think any of these kids has ever seen a white person before?" Alex asked as he took off his helmet.

"It doesn't look like it." We had about a hundred kids silently staring at us with eyes as big as the African moon.

I reached into my pocket, pulled out a piece of hard candy, and motioned to one of the little guys.

"Hey, buddy, you ever had candy?"

He looked down and shied back into the crowd behind him. Another of his bolder friends stepped forward, looking at me with wide eyes. He put out his hand and I dropped the candy into it. He quickly rejoined the group, and a dozen kids studied the foreign object.

I got their attention and then put another piece in my mouth. "You're supposed to eat it."

The boy popped it in his mouth. His face exploded with surprise like he was almost startled by the taste; then he smiled.

In no time a couple of men dressed in slacks and wearing dress shirts approached us. It turned out they were Tanzanian Seventh Day Adventist missionaries from the country's capital, Dar es Salaam, and one of them spoke English. The only English speaker in the village.

"*Jambo sana*, welcome."

"Hello, we were looking for a place we could pass the night. We have a tent. We just need a patch of ground."

"Sure, I think you could stay ova tha."

They directed us to an old, worn, concrete structure.

"Go ova tha; put your cycles ova tha."

The entire village gathered around to watch us unload our bikes. The children, absorbing our every motion and imitating every noise that came from our mouths, were especially drawn to Alex. He took out his camera, set it to flash, and held it up. They all stared at him, wondering what this silver device was. Off went the flash. A gasp, followed by silence. Some of the kids were terrified and ducked behind their older siblings. Others cheered. The adults watching in the distance chuckled. Then Alex turned the camera around and showed the closest children the picture he had just taken. Amazed and relieved, they excitedly urged him to do it again. Within two minutes, all of the village children were huddled around Alex, laughing and clapping. Alex was loving every second of it.

With the children preoccupied, Kris was able to organize our gear and set up camp—always keeping a close eye on our things. Meanwhile, I talked with the men who had led us to the site, explaining who we were and our intention.

By the time things settled down, we had stowed all our gear inside the concrete structure. Hot as it was, we had to shut the windows to our little room; if we left them open, a group of curious kids congregated outside to shamelessly gape in. We enjoyed a meal of lentils and rice with some bread that we picked up earlier that day. Then it was off to bed. Soon Kris and Alex were breathing heavy.

I lay awake, thinking, remembering.

So much to remember.

So much more to come.

BETWEEN TEETH AND BULLETS

Western Tanzania

✦

The sun was just starting to light the eastern sky. We were hoping to get underway before the village woke up, but it wasn't long before the children were awake and watching, then singing to us in unison. We hopped on our rumbling bikes and sped away. Over my shoulder I saw a hundred little boys and girls cheering and chasing us down the dirt road.

Other than a range of mountains off to the east, above which the sun had now peeked, the scenery and its colors were basically unchanged: a few different shades of green, an occasional spot of gray poking through the trees, and the narrow brown strip of dirt that continued to mark our route. We decided to stop on a fairly remote stretch, hoping to have a little peace while we enjoyed breakfast.

Our first of two meals for the day was nothing more than two pieces of old bread and one serving of oatmeal with peanut butter to be shared among the three of us. We hungrily divvied it up as a small boy wandered over to the road from the forest. He stopped thirty yards away and propped himself against his staff, staring at us as we ate. For the next twenty minutes he was our only audience. In our travels through rural Africa, large crowds of spectators had become just another part of the scenery, as common as grass or the hot sun. The color of our skin and the curious contraptions that carried us made us quite the attraction.

For the moment, having only one set of eyes studying our every motion was a welcome relief.

He silently watched us finish our last bites, stomachs still rumbling with hunger, and fire up our bikes. As soon as we pulled away he yelled, *"Eh mazungu,"* Swahili for "Hey, white man."

Today's journey was to be a comparatively short leg—just 325 km of what looked on our map to be decent road. However, we were still low on gas with no local currency. We had already emptied our jerry cans into our tanks. According to the map, the town of Sumbawanga was 75 km away. We hoped that we would be able to find gas and change money there. If not, we would have to consolidate our gas and send Alex alone with the jerry cans to the next city. He was the lightest and got the best gas mileage.

In reality, the "road"—the worst we had seen yet—was no more than an uneven dirt and rock trail with occasional wash-outs where the heavy rains had carried up to half of it away. And the dust was terrible. It was impossible to travel the road without lifting a choking cloud behind each bike. Generally two could ride side by side in the front if we rode tight, but that meant someone was always left to bring up the rear. That was the most dangerous position to be riding in because it was so difficult to make out contours in the inconsistent road through the dust. I was riding in back as the road wrapped around the side of a mountain, a steep incline to the right and a vertical drop into a ravine to the left.

We were traveling about 40 mph when we came upon a mini grand canyon about four feet wide, dropping directly into the ravine. Both Alex and I hit it. I watched his bike drop right in front of me and then catapult up into the air. I was sure he was going to crash, but somehow he managed to hang on. By the time I saw the washout, I was on top of it. There was no dodging this obstacle. I downshifted, jerked the throttle, and threw my weight back, lifting the front of the bike. My front tire just cleared the gap, but my back tire smashed the edge of the drop as it came through. It popped me straight up in the air until I felt my bike was almost vertical over my front tire. My back tire finally dropped to the ground, and I was still on the road. I couldn't help but smile. Kris saw the stunts in his mirror and turned around, throwing his fist in the air.

Yes.

The whole morning was full of equally abusive stunts, both intentional and unintentional, Kris winning the "most reckless" award.

After a couple of hours riding overloaded bikes way too fast over challenging terrain, we pulled into Sumbawanga—all wearing matching smiles. Here the streets were filled with people dressed in their finest—dresses and button shirts with ties—on their way to and from church. It was Sunday. We had completely lost track of the days. Buildings lined either side of the road, among them an open gas station. Waiting outside was a man ready to trade local currency. We bought enough currency for a couple tanks of gas and a few days of food, not sure about the rate we were getting.

Another man wandered over. "Where you going?" He spoke pretty good English.

The line was fine between getting valuable, locally known information from friendly people and walking into a con. Information had to be guarded in those parts.

"We're headed north, just touring," Alex replied.

"Oh, on doos?" motioning to our bikes.

We nodded.

"The lions, dey eat you."

"We can travel very quickly and will be off the road before nightfall," Alex assured him.

"If you don't stop, and off the road at night, maybe you make it," he chuckled.

We looked at our map. The next stretch of road was full of villages and was the only route connecting the only two cities of western Tanzania. It couldn't possibly be as bad as he was making it out to be. Besides, travel in rural Africa was unheard of. Asking the average man there about a place 100 km away would be like asking your average American for directions through China. We were waiting for him to tell us about his friend who owned a hotel or his cousin who drove a taxi. But he didn't; he just smiled and walked away.

We couldn't help but wonder. He did speak English and he didn't press the issue like we would expect from someone trying to filch a few dollars from us. We decided to take it slow and watch the villagers along the way to see how far they ventured out. They would be the ones to know when the lions were a threat.

Even if lions weren't going to be a problem, the stinging tsetse flies were. These terrible little creatures, about the size of a large horsefly, fed exclusively on blood. In just one meal they could consume twice their weight through a painful bite that feels like a bee sting and leaves a nasty welt. Worse than their sting was the ravenous disease their bite spreads. Sleeping disease, as it was called, affects both humans and animals. If not treated, it will cause death in a matter of weeks. At first its symptoms are similar to those of the flu, but the disease doesn't take long to invade the nervous system and induce a lazy, confused state (hence the name), which digresses until the infected simply lie down dead. These infectious flies were directly responsible for thousands of deaths a year in tropical Africa, and much of the poverty and hunger in the region could be credited to them. It's estimated that these flies wipe out about half the livestock in the jungles of Africa.

Our tanks were full of gas, we had money in hand, and it was only about 10 a.m.

"How far till our next stop?"

"Mpanda, just over 250 km away."

"That's all the further we're riding today?"

"That's it. We should have plenty of time."

✦

The map showed a major highway far superior to the road we had just traveled, but our naïve confidence in the map proved misguided once again. The "major highway" was nothing more than a poorly kept, seldom-traveled dirt path through the jungle. We were not making nearly the time we had hoped, but villages popped up frequently and the road was manageable. We pounded over rocks, ruts, and stumps for an hour before Kris noticed a little more motion than normal in the back of his bike. We were surrounded by the jungle.

"Did you see my duffel bouncing?" Kris hollered over the rumble of our bikes.

"Yeah, maybe something's not right with your suspension?" Alex suggested.

We stopped to investigate.

As soon as we stopped moving, a wave of greedy tsetse flies swarmed us searching for blood. The heat was unspeakable. The sun baked the humid air to a hundred and ten degrees, but we couldn't take off anything—not our black jackets, not our helmets, not our gloves. Our clothes were quickly saturated, and sweat began to stream down our faces, chests, and backs.

Kris lay on his back under the bike. "You are not going to believe this," he said. "The frame is cracked all the way through!"

I crouched to see, looking up under the luggage rack. "Oh crap."

Alex took a deep breath. "This will be an interesting one."

None of us thought for a second that we couldn't fix it.

Fortunately, after a while the flies seemed to leave us more or less alone. As long as no one started his engine we could take off our helmets, even our jackets for a while. For reasons I can't explain, they seemed to be particularly fond of a running engine, even more so if it was moving.

"Hey guys, my frame's cracking too," Alex said.

"Mine's not cracked, but it's showing wear," I said. "We had better take it easy, huh?"

We were prepared to make just about any roadside repair, but a broken frame—this was a tough one. We needed a welder, something we would not see again until we reached Mpanda, now about 160 km away. On a good day it would take us two hours to get there. As a temporary fix we tried to wire the frame in place. Really, the only thing directly affected by the crack was Kris's ability to carry a load. As long as we stopped the piece from vibrating and lightened his load, it should be okay. We baked for another hour or so while we reinforced the frame with everything we could come up with: scrap metal to cuff the crack, another piece to line the crack along the inside. When we were confident that it would hold, Alex and I took all the heavy objects, leaving Kris with as little gear as possible.

We pressed on. Not so much as another set of tire tracks appeared on the rugged trail. It was lunchtime, and we hadn't progressed nearly as far toward Mpanda as we had hoped. So much for a quick, easy stretch—but honestly, what does quick and easy even mean in the jungles of Africa? To turn around at this point would have been just as far as to finish the day's ride, and the wire job seemed to be working. Always the optimists, we kept going.

Please let that thing hold until we get to Mpanda.

Another forty-five minutes of rocks and stumps went by, and all looked well. Then we saw it, ever so slight, almost unnoticeable if we hadn't been looking: the back end of Kris's bike was bouncing again. The wire fix had come undone. We stopped in a bustling little village to make the repair, hoping the tsetse flies wouldn't be as bad in the heavily populated clearing.

Immediately a crowd of about sixty people surrounded us, harmlessly staring. We inspected the damage. The wire had busted and it looked like the crack had gotten worse.

"I'll go see if I can find us a bite to eat," I said, somewhat disappointed by my unanswered prayer.

Alex reclined on his bike, comfortably resting on his duffel. Kris stripped his bike of all unnecessary parts and began to labor away.

The crowd watched.

⁂

I wandered up to the market, a relatively small area with open walls. The roof was made of sun-dried bamboo stalks tied together, with green banana leaves thrown on top; vertical bamboo stalks strategically placed every so often supported the roof. It did a good job keeping the sun out of the market area and was surprisingly cool considering the intense heat of the day and all the bodies fighting for a place in the shade. I wandered through the dusty walkways lined on both sides by vendors, all selling the same three items: brown dried fish, bananas, and old worn-out clothes. It seemed to me that the latter were the most coveted possessions in the market. The majority of the people were literally wearing rags. Around the market little boys ran and played. Like most other African children we had encountered so far, they too owned only one article of clothing, maybe just a ripped sweater or equally tattered pair of shorts. I had been warned to not even wear sandals because of all the vicious parasites that could bore through the skin, yet these swollen-hollow-bellied children sat with naked bottoms in the dirt.

Alex strolled over to see how the food hunt was going.

"We've got bananas."

Over in the corner we noticed a woman roasting corn over a charcoal fire.

"That'll make a pretty good little lunch."

Alex grabbed a few bananas as I waited for three ears of corn to cook.

Back at the center of the crowd, Kris seemed to be finishing up. His face was less confident than before. "That should hold it . . . I hope."

Please let that hold; we don't have time for another repair and none of us has the energy for another night in the bush. Please let that hold till Mpanda, I said out loud inside my helmet—knowing fully well that it wouldn't.

At times like this in life I usually found myself asking why. *Why do people do this? Why do we invite trials, frustrations, and discomfort? Why do we intentionally put ourselves in situations that we know will push us beyond where we like to be pushed, to places we know will be tough?*

Maybe, I finally resolved, there isn't one simple answer, just a longing to be tested and proven. A desire to know that we can overcome whatever obstacle we may be forced to face. It is only when we are pushed past our self-perceived limits that we are able to clearly see our truest nature, discover our deepest selves; only then can we hope to improve upon what we find. To do so is neither safe nor comfortable, it is both dangerous and scary. But we warriors at heart were meant to live dangerously.

That day I saw it in myself firsthand. Adversity tempers us.

Our journey through Africa thus far had been full of both joy and trials. Often the two came intertwined. Today on this road was such a time. I was thrilled to be with my best friends in such a beautiful land, but at the same time the only thing I could think about was getting through today, moving on to the next place.

The wire broke again. Two more grueling hours stopped in the baking heat, battling the evil flies.

"Hey, Erik, do you have any more water?" Alex asked. "I'm out."

"I drank my reserve an hour ago. Keep your eyes open for a stream."

Please, just a little farther.

We were back on the road for only thirty kilometers before yet another breakdown and three more torturous hours of repairs. *Will this day never end?*

The sun was getting lower. Mpanda was still at least 100 km away and we hadn't seen a village in hours. The map listed several villages along this stretch, but we saw nothing but empty jungle. Perhaps they, like our patience, had been consumed by the sun.

We spread out quite a bit, trying to keep the dust down. Challenging terrain meant the occasional crash was unavoidable. One particularly rough stretch got the best of me and I crashed quickly. Kris was riding behind me.

"You all right, Erik?"

"I'm fine. Let's keep moving."

Alex and Kris switched bikes, Kris taking the heavier of the two as he weighed fifteen pounds more than Alex and was a lot taller. Kris and I were riding in back, with Alex speeding up ahead, when we noticed a couple bolts in the road as we drove by. Then we saw the metal plate that had been mounted on the back of his bike lying on the path. The wire job must have broken again. We raced ahead to tell Alex before more damage was done. As we ripped around the next corner there he sat in the road, dismounting Kris's bike. The rack had broken off completely. The excess vibration had rattled a couple crucial bolts loose, spilling what he was carrying all over the ground. The bike was out of commission for the time being. We pulled up next to Kris's bike and stopped, inviting a wave of winged beasts.

"We need a welder. Where are we?" I asked, frustrated and angry that one more pleading with God had gone unanswered. No sooner than we started to make some real progress toward our destination, something else broke and delayed us again.

Kris looked at a more general map of the region and pointed to the middle of a big green area south of Mpanda labeled Katavi National Park and Game Reserve.

"It looks like we're right about here."

The words of the man from the gas station at Sumbawanga began to ring in my head. "The lions, dey eat you. If you don't stop, and off the road at night, maybe you make it."

Here it was just before sunset, and we were stuck indefinitely right in the middle of a national park that was famous for lion spotting. Apparently the most unique and attractive quality of this particular stretch was that at night the lions all came to the road. Because it was so wet in this jungle, and normally lions live in dryer brush, the beasts traveled on the road at night to avoid having to walk through the tall wet grass when the dew settled. This allowed intrepid (or uninformed) visitors the opportunity to observe truly wild lions—unlike those in the Massi Mara of eastern Tanzania—that were otherwise almost impossible to spot. This would have been an awesome place to drive through at night in the back of a Land Rover (or in a tank for that matter).

One of the reasons we wanted to take dirt bikes through Africa was to fully experience it—not through a pane of glass, but up close and personal. The notion seemed much less romantic now as we sat hungry and sweating on the side of the road, counting the minutes we had before the lions came out to play. We put the map aside and inspected the bike.

"With some work we could make it rideable at slow speeds. But it won't be able to carry a duffel," Kris announced. "And it will take some time even to fix it that much."

"Even if we could get it fixed tonight, we can't carry all our gear on just two bikes" noted Alex. "And look at your bike, Erik! The seam of your duffel's ripped out."

"What?" I looked, and sure enough the back of my bag was wide open and I had been spilling clothes and even a couple tools for the last, who-knew how far. It must have torn when I crashed. I couldn't believe we didn't notice it sooner.

"Perfect, absolutely perfect. Could things get any better?"

The situation looked grim. We were stranded—out of food, out of water. And I was tired of begging God.

"So we've got two options. We either leave our gear here and try to make it to Mpanda riding all night, or we sit tight and fend off lions all night," I said.

"The chances that we'll ever find our bags again if we leave them in this jungle are slim. Everything looks the same here," Kris interrupted.

"We have already been riding for ten exhausting hours with no real break and just some oatmeal, a dry ear of corn, and a banana to eat. How long will it take us to get to Mpanda? Two hours, ten hours? We might not make it at all, then we'd be stuck on the lion's road with no gear," I continued. "I say we stay here and wait for morning. We'll build a big fire just off the road and take turns standing watch.

"Alex and I will get some firewood and start setting up camp, but let's get the bikes ready to go just in case we need to get out of here."

I hoped huddling our sleeping bags around the fire would be enough to keep the lions away. Two could sleep while the third kept watch, armed with a hatchet and a spotlight. The plan was less than ideal, but what else could we do?

No one was excited about spending another night in the bush. We were already dead tired, and now it looked like it would be at least another day until we would be able to eat and rest.

Our frustration was mounting; you could almost smell it. The monkeys in the trees chattered at us mockingly. The tsetse flies swarmed us, looking for an exposed patch of skin from which to feed.

+

Another torturous hour passed. The sun had set, the color was fading from the sky, and it was getting difficult to see. This was the time when the animals came to life. During the day the jungle seems such a beautiful, peaceful place; the beasts to whom the jungle belongs rest in the shade. But after dark the jungle erupts. Lions prowl, elephants run through the trees, baboons wreak havoc. It all takes place behind the blackness, betrayed by the occasional roar or breaking of branches. You can only guess what is lurking just a few feet away.

"That should do it if we go slow," Kris predicted.

His bike was rideable at slow speeds with no load. Good. We could make a break for it if we needed, but how would we get all of our gear to Mpanda? Whatever. That was tomorrow's challenge.

Just as we were preparing to dig in for the night, we noticed something. Through the quickly fading twilight, we saw a speck of white bouncing down the road in the distance.

"What's that?" At first I could barely make it out. "Could it be a truck?" We hadn't seen another vehicle on this road since Sumbawanga.

It got bigger and bigger. We recognized it. It was a Land Cruiser! Kris stepped into the road and stopped the vehicle while Alex and I rushed to the window.

"Hello, do you speak English?"

The driver just stared at us blankly. The wave of flies that had been following the Land Cruiser caught up and was upon us.

Then the man sitting next to him leaned over and shouted, "Hallo, yes, I speak English. What are you doing here?" He had a callus on his forehead, something shared by all devout Muslims from touching their head to the ground during prayer. He was obviously a spiritual man; maybe he would help us.

"How far is it to the next welder?" I asked.

"Ohhh, very far. Is a long ways."

"Where is the next village?"

"Very far, long ways," he repeated, squinting his eyes and waving his hand to the north.

"Very far doesn't mean too much to us; we've come four thousand kilometers and have another ten thousand to go," I snapped, though I knew that the occupants of this vehicle could be our only hope.

Alex spoke up. He asked the man his name. Sbaa, the man answered—the Arabic word for the number seven. Alex patiently explained to Sbaa our situation and asked if it would be possible for us to throw our bags into the back of the vehicle while we followed him to Mpanda, the only stop on this road. The Good Samaritan, Sbaa, and his ever-so-kind driver agreed to help us. We threw all our excess weight into the back of the truck. Sbaa and his driver nervously swatted at the tsetse flies, then quickly jumped back into the Land Cruiser, relieved to have something between them and the insects. Sbaa cracked his window and yelled, "Follow us."

They continued to push down the road as we hopped on our bikes and quickly caught up. The jungle was black; to either side of the road all you could see was the outline of the trees against the starry night; in front, only what fell between our headlights and the three red taillights of the Land Cruiser guiding us from ahead.

I couldn't believe it. Here we were in the middle of the jungle, stranded, hopeless, all alone, and out of nowhere comes a man who not only spoke English but was also willing to help us. He might as well have been an angel. It was still going to be a long night; we had at least 100 km to go and we were already nearly beaten to death. But at least we would not have to fight off lions. We had hope and we had a goal. Sometimes that's all you need. If we were lucky, we would be able to rest in a bed tonight—with a full stomach.

The road was grueling. We had to battle rock, sand, and ruts every kilometer. Our stallions were as broken and tired as we were. Alex's bike was the first to go. Kris and I were riding side by side talking (something that could only be done at low speeds) when Alex hit something in the road, swerved sharp to the right, and took a nasty crash into a big hole. I rushed over to him and ditched my bike. He was down about six feet with his foot pinned under his bike. He was struggling for air.

I jumped down to him as Kris lifted the bike off his foot.

"Hey, you all right?"

He choked a couple of breaths.

"Yeah. Just knocked the wind out of me. Give me a sec."

He breathed, just breathed and nothing more, for a few moments. Then he slowly got up. It looked to me like he hit his head pretty hard.

"Whoa, what was that? I was just driving straight, I hit a little rut, and my bike shot out from under me."

Kris inspected Alex's bike while I inspected Alex. Nothing was broken, but he did have a bad headache and felt like vomiting. It looked like a concussion, but to be honest, Kris and I both felt similar, what with hardly anything to eat or drink all day.

"Hey, Erik, look at this," Kris shouted.

Alex's steering was so loose that the bolt holding it together was ready to fall off. In addition to that, his exhaust pipe had broken off and his front rim had been bent badly in the crash. Countless other bolts had vibrated loose as well.

Sbaa and his driver had noticed that we weren't behind them and turned around. We took our tools and tightened everything as best as we could given the circumstances and inspected the other bikes. My steering was also loose and several bolts were ready to fall out at the next bump in the road. Kris's didn't look any worse than it had a couple hours earlier, but that wasn't really saying much. We threw Alex's hot exhaust pipe into the back of the Land Cruiser as Sbaa nervously scanned for lions and elephants. Alex was hurting; he took my bike. It was in the best shape of the three. Kris took Alex's bike, which still sort of ran, just very loudly. I rode in back on Kris's bike, acting as a sort of cleanup man. We had a hurt rider on a good bike, a good rider on a hurt bike, and me trailing, ready to pick up whichever of the two broke down first.

An elephant trumpeted to my left, not a stone's throw away, yet I couldn't see it so black was the night. On the ground I saw fresh lion tracks in the sand. Animals were there, on either side of us, before and behind. We could sense their presence, hear their savage screams; we knew they were watching us as we slowly passed, barely moving down the road. The bikes couldn't take the terrain any faster in the condition they were in.

For the first time on our journey I was afraid. Not startled, like how a charging elephant will make you feel. I mean a bone-chilling, deep fear. I was afraid of the dark, of the monsters hiding there, of another crash, of a million things waiting to harm us—but it was more than that. Sure, I was aware of the immediate dangers we were facing, but my fear came from beyond. I had a disconcerting sense that all was not well. We were unwelcome strangers in this place, with no idea how much longer we had to travel before we reached Mpanda.

The night continued like this for three more hours—fighting the jungle, fighting to keep our balance, fighting to stay awake, to keep going for just another kilometer.

Followed by another.

Another.

Another.

We lost all concept of time; minutes dragged on for hours; hours took days to pass. The sun should have come up by now. I hung over the handlebars far behind the rest, waiting for the next crash. Alex must have been so tired. I could barely keep going and I hadn't taken that fall. Kris was negotiating not only his fatigue, but also a bike that threatened to stop running at any moment. Mpanda became a myth, a fairytale in my mind. It was a place that existed only in dreams. I didn't actually expect to ever arrive.

But then peeking through the jungle was a light. At first I questioned whether or not it was even real. It was just a glimpse, just a spark. The road wrapped around one more bend, and sure enough there it was: Mpanda, our refuge, our rest.

We followed the white Land Cruiser through the small town, down dark dusty roads to a guesthouse. The Good Samaritan did all the negotiating; we merely sat on our bikes reassuring each other that our journey was over for the day.

"You have a room here."

Like lifeless zombies we grabbed our bags out of the back of the Land Cruiser and lugged them down the narrow hallway to a room with two beds. Heaven. Here we would be able to rest for a few days, nurse ourselves back to health, and get our bikes ready for another demanding stretch of road.

"We must go now; the restaurant"—there was only one in Mpanda—"is about to close," Sbaa said to us.

We compliantly got back on our bikes. Alex, too beat to ride, climbed onto the back of mine. We followed our friend to the restaurant and ate as much gristly goat meat and rice as we could fit into our stomachs.

Back at the guesthouse, we slept soundly in our beds for what was left of the night and through most of the next day.

Little did we know of the chaos that had passed through the town just hours before us and the turmoil happening around us.

Mud was a common adversary.

BETTER THAN MTV

Northwestern Tanzania

✦

I awoke with the sun, already high above the horizon, shining through our window. Alex and Kris were still lying peacefully on their mats, Alex just to my side; Kris across the room seven feet away. I grabbed my journal and stepped out into a paved courtyard littered with cheap white plastic lawn furniture. Immediately I felt uneasy as several concerned eyes looked up to meet my gaze. They said nothing, nor I to them as I walked out of the guesthouse and into the dusty side lot where we had left our tired and broken bikes the night before. Passersby stared at me accusingly as they walked by our bikes and me.

"Hey, what are you doing up so early?" Kris asked as he stumbled out the front door.

"It's almost 10:30, hardly early."

"It's all relative, Erik; ask Einstein."

"Alex still sleeping?"

"Yeah, he was pretty sound asleep. I heard you get up."

"How do the bikes look?"

"They're gonna need some love but nothing we shouldn't be able to fix."

Kris and I explored the area surrounding the guesthouse in search of something to eat. A stand selling fresh sugarcane was the only thing open.

"What's going on here? Why is everything closed?"

"I don't know. It's kinda creepy.

"Hello. Do you speak English?" I asked a visibly disturbed woman behind the stack of sugarcane. She just stared at me anxiously. I smiled and tossed her sixty Tanzanian shillings (about five cents) and helped myself to two pieces of the sweet stalk.

Kris whipped out his knife and shaved off the tough green outer revealing the soft sweet core.

"Hey, can you cut mine open?"

Just then Kris sliced through the other piece of sugarcane and right through his hand, opening a deep gash on the inside of his left index finger.

"Shoot."

"That looks pretty deep. Do you want to go back and fix it up?"

"Nah, I'm good. Let's figure out what's going on in this town."

A nicely dressed man briskly walked out of the guesthouse and was passing us indifferently on the street, obviously not in the mood to talk.

"Hello. Excuse me, sir."

"Yes?"

"Do you speak English?"

"Yes," he answered, visibly annoyed.

"What's going on here? Why is everyone so upset?"

"You don't know what happened the last night?" he asked, looking down at Kris's hand, which was now dripping blood onto the ground. Kris self-consciously moved it out of view behind his back.

"The gunman come tru and kill the people!" And quickly the man explained to us what had happened the night prior.

Just after sunset, as the town went about its usual business, terror had struck. Shop owners were cleaning up for the day. The cafes were filling as people huddled around televisions to watch European soccer matches on satellite TV. The restaurant was busy, serving a full dining room—their choice of either boney chicken and rice or goat gristle and rice—when they heard gunfire.

A man came wandering up the street with a loaded AK-47 and a bottle of booze, apparently wanting money and some form of transportation. He casually walked up to a taxi driver sitting in his car waiting for the next customer to emerge from the restaurant, lifted his gun to the open window, and shot the driver right through the head. People started to run as he pulled the lifeless driver out of his car. The gunman looked around him for his next victim. The people in the restaurant watched helplessly through the window as he stared each of them down, surveying the scene, and then strolled over to a nearby shop. Inside the shop owner was hiding behind the counter. A couple of rounds into the old man and he died quietly. The gunman helped himself to the money and whatever else pleased him and wandered back over to the now empty taxi and drove away. Word had it he had fled to Burundi and would almost certainly never be apprehended.

"This happened last night?" Kris asked in amazement.

"Yes, it happen just last night. The people is dead going to be buried now. TOO MUCH this happen!" The man turned around and without a good-bye continued down the street.

"Kris, we would have been in that restaurant last night at sunset."

He just stared at me, speechless.

"We would have been the only three 'rich' white men for hundreds of miles. With three motorcycles sitting outside that restaurant where we were enjoying dinner, we would have been a winning lottery ticket for the gunman."

"If we hadn't broken down we would have been right there."

Kris's bleeding hand snapped me back.

"Your hand, is it okay?"

"It looks like I cut it pretty good," he said, holding it up to examine. "It's gonna need stitches."

"Let's fix it up," I said as we headed back to the guesthouse to grab some iodine, thread, and a needle.

Getting the first-aid-kit out of the room must have woken Alex. He wandered into the courtyard and through a big yawn saw me stabbing at Kris's bloody hand with a dull needle and thread. Kris was gritting his teeth trying not to make too much noise.

"Can't I leave you two alone for five minutes?" Alex asked. "Are you okay, Kris?"

"Just a flesh wound," Kris answered. I dropped the needle and gave my brother a big hug.

"What's going on, Erik?"

"You'll never believe what happened last night while we were crashed on the side of the road."

✦

Our bikes were in bad shape: frames cracked, bolts loose, rims badly bent out of shape, air filters full of a fine brown sludge, just to mention a few problems. It would take us a couple days to make them rideable again. We borrowed an oxyacetylene welder from a small metalsmith shop and completely stripped down our bikes to the raw frame. The local metalsmiths were excited to explore our bikes and see how we would go about fixing them. They even helped with several tasks free of charge. We reinforced every crack in the frames. We unscrewed and put back every bolt with locking washers and Locktite. We hammered bent rims straight. We changed out air filters. Our bikes were like bulletproof tanks by the time we were done with them. No rough road would hurt them now.

We had rested a couple days, eaten well, and were ready to go. Several of the shop owners and metalsmiths with whom we had become acquainted joined us for a celebratory dinner the night before we left. They were as proud of our reconditioned bikes as we were. We woke up early the next morning and mounted our steeds, leaving a large group waving good-bye and wishing us safe travels. Back to the only road, traveling north.

In less than a mile we were in the jungle again. It was so beautiful. Every inch of ground was covered with life; everywhere you looked was some unique shade of green. Ancient trees wound their way toward the sky; their broad branches, filled with birds, looked like the perfect napping spot for a leopard. The rest was six-foot-tall grass, and one could only imagine what was hiding in its cover. Such a mysterious place.

I was overwhelmed with the feeling that we were venturing into a realm undiscovered by the modern world. If that was not entirely true, surely we must have been doing it in a way that had never been done before. No one else would be this crazy. We had no chase van offering parts and repairs. We had no bus ready to take us to the airport if things didn't work out. We had no plan B. We had no safety net. One way or another we had to get through the next six hundred miles. We were traveling right into the darkest part of Africa, a place where no laws existed to protect us, where nothing was against the rules. We were headed right into the center of the madness, right into the serenity that exists therein. And all we had to rely on to get out was each other, and God's grace.

I listened to the hum of my bike and felt the power in my right hand. I couldn't contain myself. I screamed inside my helmet:

"Thank you, God! I can't believe that I get to live this life!"

But suddenly the road—and our progress—fell apart. The dirt two-track between the middle of nowhere and the clear white spot on the map turned into a giant sand trap. Our bikes, fully loaded, weighed about five hundred pounds plus the weight of the rider. Sand is a tough obstacle to negotiate on two wheels. You twist the throttle, but the bike just kicks sideways; you lose your balance, you fall. Sand finds its way into your clothes. It gets in your boots and in your socks. It sticks to your sweaty skin. Your clothes turn into sandpaper.

We all had our days to wipe out, and this day was mine. Every time Kris and Alex turned around I was on my butt in the sand, cursing my bike. My cooling fan wasn't working for some reason, so the bike overheated often. We crawled through that oceanless beach, engines revved, clutches gripping.

Finally, we painstakingly found the end of the sand and had an open dirt path. A cloud covered the sun, offering us our first shade of the day. It felt divine.

"It looks like there's rain in that cloud."

"A little rain wouldn't feel half bad."

I should have known better by now.

The clouds grew and darkened. They looked furious. We hadn't gone more than ten miles before the sky opened and unleashed a torrential downpour.

We parked the bikes close together and got under a tarp, but it didn't do much to keep us dry. We were all soaked. Just an hour ago I was worried about dehydration and heat stroke, now I was fighting not to get cold. I looked at Alex. He was fifteen pounds lighter than me and had been negotiating the same heavy load through the grueling sand. Now he was visibly shaking, but he didn't say a word about it. He just reached into his pocket and broke open a pouch of peanuts. He offered Kris and me a handful.

"Where did you get those?" I inquired.

"Oh, I picked them up a few days ago."

"You've had them this whole time and didn't even tell us about them?" I thought back to our days of hunger on the road.

"Yeah, well if I had told you, you would have eaten them and we wouldn't have them now."

I couldn't help but smile.

Alex divvied up his secret stash three ways.

The rain rescued us from the heat but posed a whole new set of problems, the worst of which was that the packed dirt had turned into icy-slick clay. Huge puddles were everywhere. We were only able to go another ten miles or so after the rain stopped; even then progress was slow and keeping the wheels under us almost impossible. Kris fell, so I parked my bike to help. As I walked over to him, my bike slid down all by itself and fell over, breaking the mirror and clutch handle mount.

I wondered if we were ever going to make it. This was the most intense, brutal, unforgiving place I had ever been in my life. After six hours up against the road and the elements we had covered only seventy-five miles and reentered raw jungle. It looked just like in the movies. Wide open grassy fields with islands of trees. Green stacked on green stacked on green and big boulders lying all about. Breathtaking mountains and valleys. Waterfalls, monkeys, exotic birds. We hadn't passed one village or seen one other vehicle since Mpanda. We were all alone, lost in the middle of nowhere. We were free.

We stumbled upon and set up camp beside a ruined house that looked like it had been built a half-century earlier by some European searching for solitude. It sat atop the peak of a ridge just off the road and overlooked a huge valley with a vista of nothing but jungle green as far as you could see. I doubt anyone had been there in over a decade. A tranquil stream nearby provided us a place to bathe. The sun was going down.

Because we had hoped to be in Kigoma tonight, our food rations were limited. At least we had a decent breakfast of bread and liver back in Mpanda. Tonight's ration was a half pound of rice, one can of beans, and a cup of lentils all split three ways. Alex and I got firewood while Kris prepared the meal. After dinner we sat around the fire and reminisced about the day. The worst days always made for the best campfires. Alex and I had found some great firewood, the heart of which was a brilliant red and so hard that a single log burned for an hour.

Lots of time to sit. Lots of time to talk.

The last embers of the fire were flickering a dull orange. The tent was calling us.

We were tired, but we slept light. Unsure.

Alex woke up in the middle of the night and needed to pee. As he got up, about to unzip the tent, he heard a growl nearby and wisely decided to hold it until morning. The commotion woke Kris and a few minutes later he was up, needing to take care of some urgent business. He groggily stumbled outside, found himself a nice clearing, and popped a squat. As he was finishing he heard something just through the wall of tall grass. Lifting his little flashlight he saw big red eyes about four feet off the ground watching him. Whatever beast the eyes belonged to moved out of sight and a terrified Kris ran back into the tent. No one else left the tent until the sun was high the following morning, but I finally had to get out there to fix my broken radiator fan—a blown fuse buried under the gas tank turned out to be the culprit. I opened the tent and was greeted with lion tracks, baboon tracks, and others that I couldn't identify.

✦

We didn't get on the road until after 11 a.m. The first twenty miles or so were tough, but the road got better and better the closer we got to Kigoma. As the roads got better and other vehicles got more frequent, the drivers got worse. At one point some terrible Tanzanian driver ran all three of us off the road.

Seven hours later we arrived in Kigoma. The people didn't like our being there for some reason. As we drove into the city, little kids pretended to shoot us with imaginary guns while the adults stared at us with angry eyes and waved for us to turn around and leave. When we finally parked at a market, a man came up to us demanding money. When we refused, a crowd formed. One man, who was clearly crazy, ripped his shirt off and into little pieces and began to belligerently circle us. We started up the bikes, gunned through the mob, and drove until we found a fenced-in guesthouse on the shore of Lake Tanganyika. It was a little more expensive than what we were hoping to pay, but the security was worth every shilling.

Our time in Kigoma was restful. We spent a couple of days there doing absolutely nothing but relaxing. We talked, swam, and ate—and did our best to avoid the malaria-carrying mosquitoes, though an occasional bite was inevitable. Kigoma was the first place we had been that even resembled civilization since leaving South Africa. It felt like any border city, full of outlaws and problems; but we were comfortable in our little sanctuary.

The only place in the entire city of Kigoma where Internet service was available was in the one "nice" hotel on a bluff outside town. There we paid the outrageous five American dollars per hour to check our email and connect with our contacts in Burundi.

The border to Burundi at Kigoma was usually closed to travelers, but we had managed to acquire visas that would let us enter for a month. That didn't change the fact that finding a hotel or guesthouse would be nearly impossible in Burundi. Camping was out of the question as well. Burundi was in the middle of a terrible civil war; and though it looked like things were starting to settle with the UN's presence, everyone we talked to warned us about how dangerous and fragile the situation was just a few miles further north. We wouldn't even think about crossing that border until we knew where we were going, that the road was passable, and that our contacts were expecting us.

While we were sitting in the semi-luxurious resort—surely the only one of its kind for hundreds of kilometers—we saw a group of white people come through the doors, the first white people we had seen since Zambia. They had loads of North Face duffel bags (the same ones that we had strapped to our bikes) and were carrying camera equipment.

"Hey, what's going on?"

"Oh, we're with MTV. We're filming a show here." And off they walked.

"Huh, that's weird," Alex said, as I continued our work on the Internet.

A few moments later we looked up as another group came through the doors. A couple of the faces looked familiar, but I didn't think much of it. They wandered around the lobby, and Alex, always ready to make new acquaintances, overheard someone talking about the Serengeti.

"How was that? We're hoping to travel to the Serengeti too." Alex was casually talking to this guy who introduced himself as Jimmy.

I looked at Kris. "Isn't that the guy from *Saturday Night Live*? Jimmy Fallon?"

"Yeah, I think it might be."

"And was that Cameron Diaz and Justin Timberlake over there?"

"Huh, I thought Cameron Diaz was taller than that; and that guy has a little bit of a gut. Isn't Justin Timberlake skinny?"

"What are they doing here?"

I joined Alex to see what was going on while Kris continued to work away at the computer.

"Jimmy, this is my brother Erik."

"Good to meet you. Hey, do you guys know if there is any place I can get a drink around here? Is there any good nightlife?"

We laughed and answered in unison: "No."

Alex and Jimmy got to talking about the program that MTV was filming. Jimmy asked Alex how we had found our way to this remote corner of the world. Alex explained our journey up to this point—about struggling to get dirt bikes and then of our travels from Cape Town—and about where we planned on going from here.

Jimmy was absolutely speechless. He just stared at Alex, with that unmistakable wonder and longing in his eyes. "Wow," he said. "I'd love to do something like that."

"Hey, Erik," Alex interjected, "did you get in touch with our friends in Burundi?"

"Yeah, I told them we'd be there tomorrow."

"We had better get going then; we've got a little bit of work to do before we get underway. It was nice to meet you, Jimmy."

"I've heard Burundi is a pretty rough place. Good luck, you guys," Jimmy said.

Kris strolled over from the computer.

"Well, let's giddyup."

We left first thing the next morning.

The road to the border was a beautiful little dirt track wrapping through the hills. To our left towered jagged green mountains brushed by clouds. Every now and then we got a glimpse of silvery Lake Tanganyika behind us. Anything would grow in this ground, any crop at all, yet we saw only grass. For the first time in days we were not alone on the road. A big white vehicle that looked like a UPS truck was wallowing in the knee-deep mud alongside us. We battled for every inch of progress, but it was a battle we were used to fighting.

We entered Burundi without incident and stopped at the Burundi immigration and customs offices. Everything was in French. As usual I did the talking, but my command of the French language lay somewhere between terrible and nonexistent.

"Où sont vos passeports?" an angry official asked us.

"What? Oh. *Ici.*" I handed him our passports and Carnets.

"Où sont vos visas?"

"Ici."

"Où allez-vous?" he asked, looking at our documents.

"Bujumbura."

"La route ferme à quatre heures. Les militaires fouillent la campagne environnante pour les rebelles. Personne n'entre ou laisse la ville après quatre heures."

"Hey guys, I think he just told me that the city closes at 4 p.m."

"Say what?"

"I didn't catch it all, but he said something about rebels and closing the city at four." I turned back to the man to verify. *"Nous arrivons là auparavant quatre est bon?"*

"Arrivez là avant que quatre heures ou vous avez de grands problèmes."

"We have to get there by four," I said to Kris and Alex. I didn't need to say more. Any moron could understand "grands problèmes."

If the map was right and all went well, Bujumbura was a four-hour ride. It was now ten o'clock. We had only a two-hour cushion.

We collected our stamped passports and Carnets and walked outside back to our bikes.

"We can make it; let's go," Kris said.

Alex looked at his watch and then at me.

"Well, there's no turning back now. This visa's only good once," I said.

Alex nodded his head. "Let's get going then."

No Candy Shop

Burundi

By the river in Burundi, just after Alex pelted the hippo. He's still holding the slingshot.

Burundi, the place where order ends. It made Kigoma look like a candy shop. Leaving Tanzania and entering Burundi was like going from the familiar streets of Michigan to Bosnia. Every few hundred meters stood men with AK-47s casually thrown over their shoulders. Machine gun turrets had their barrels trained on us as we motored past. Police stops were everywhere. Big armored personnel carriers with 50-caliber machine guns mounted on top and "UN" painted on the sides were packed full of soldiers with signature blue helmets. The military here were different than we had seen in the other countries we had traveled through. They looked harsh. These men had used their weapons; they had killed. I could see it in their eyes. Just like the Moroccan military man who had threatened to shoot my refugee friends and me the first time I was arrested on Gurugu.

Reactions from the rest of the people varied. Some were excited to see our motorcycles, cheering and waving. Others appeared upset by our presence. All were taken off guard and somewhat confused as we drove by.

The rebels in Burundi moved at night. Since the UN showed up, there had been fewer attacks, but the situation was still extremely volatile. The country was voting on a new constitution the next day. Depending on the outcome, it could be a step toward resolution—or a leap back into war. Times were tense and likely to get worse before they got better.

We needed to connect with our contacts that very night. They were waiting for us in the only real city left: Burundi's capital, Bujumbura. We reached Bujumbura around 2:30, an hour and a half before they locked down the city and swept the surrounding hills for suspicious activity. Too close for comfort but we made it nonetheless.

The city was in chaos. Dozens of people were whistling and hollering at us, trying to detain us as we passed. We needed to stop. We needed to call our contacts.

I spotted a telebotique across the road. Kris and Alex read my mind and we stopped in unison in a little dirt patch just off the road. A crowd of twenty was upon us before I could even get off my bike. They all wanted what they didn't have: our things, our bikes, our passports, our skin color. They wanted out.

"Go make that call, but be snappy about it," Kris hollered over the crowd. "Alex and I will handle the crowd."

I went, I called, I got the plan.

The crowd had doubled in the two minutes I was gone.

"Let's move, Erik. Time to go," Alex shouted to me. I jumped on the bike and we burst through the now somewhat aggressive throng.

Some followed us but didn't have a chance of catching us. We were safe on our bikes.

"Someone's going to meet us in front of the UN headquarters in ten minutes. It's supposed to be on this street, so keep your eyes open."

"Up there on the left."

"Let's keep moving and burn some time."

"Good call."

I was starting to seriously wonder what kind of hard-core, die-hard Christian called this city home. We spent about seven or eight minutes circling the compound before we pulled over again. A crowd was already headed toward us before we even stopped. This time Kris swung around and parked between Alex and me, facing opposite us—just so we could keep our eyes on every angle.

"They should be here any minute. But if things start to heat up, rip through this crowd. Don't stop until you're through it, no matter what."

Alex nodded his head.

The band drew closer. The air grew tense.

Just then a SUV with tinted windows pulled up and, without stopping, signaled for us to follow. Our bikes still running and ready to bust through the unflinching wall of opportunists, we followed the SUV to a gated home. A couple of locals were working the fence. It felt good to have the fence close behind us with our bikes safely inside.

The passenger door of the SUV swung open and a skinny boy no more than fourteen hopped down. "Hi, I'm Austin."

Out of the driver's side a petite but dignified woman with a small voice greeted us. "Hey, guys, I'm Tambry. My husband, Dan, should be back soon. He's doing some business. You sure know how to draw a crowd, don't ya? Come on in. I'll get you something to drink."

Dan and Tambry worked for an organization called World Relief and initiated micro-enterprise centers in the middle of some of the world's toughest spots. They welcomed us into their home like we were family.

We went to sleep early, the whole spacious floor of a room all to ourselves. We felt safe here. But elections were tomorrow.

The morning sunlight was bouncing off the windowsill. I could hear a bird outside welcoming the new day with a song. I could smell a pot of coffee brewing out in the kitchen. For a moment I forgot where I was.

"Did you hear the gunshots last night?" Alex was already sitting up. Kris was fighting to stay asleep.

"What? No."

"It sounded like someone went through a few mags up in the mountains."

"I heard 'em," Kris said, still half asleep.

No one else said a thing about it all morning. I guess it was a common noise here at night.

It was a hot and cloudy day, the kind when you can't see the sun but you still need to squint. We had a lot of tuning up to do on our bikes. Dan took us to an orphanage run by some other missionaries. They had a grinder and a welder with a huge pile of scrap metal. It was going to take a couple days, but we'd be able to touch up the job we did in Mpanda.

As we were leaving the orphanage, I heard a child shrieking. I looked over to see a pack of dogs chasing a little boy of about eight—jumping up on him, nipping at his rear. He fell down. His screams became even more intense, piercing my skin and driving straight through my bones. The pack buried their snouts into the boy's flesh.

Dan ran over and kicked off the dogs. Just twenty yards away a soldier armed with an AK and a couple of potato masher grenades stood by, seemingly enjoying the scene. No one else even turned a head.

I had seen poverty, people who live and die with nothing; last year's work in Morocco accustomed me to such suffering. But in Burundi I saw something that I had never seen before. War was in your face all the time, everywhere you looked. The people here were poor, yes. They lived without what we consider bare survival essentials—but it was more than that. Uncertainty loomed over their heads every day. War had come and gone and come again more times than they cared to count. I don't imagine a person alive in this city had not lost someone.

We kept busy working on the bikes. We had a simple list of parts we needed—just basic steel bolts. I hopped in an old rusty Land Cruiser with a person whose association with the orphanage was vague—a thirtysomething guy in a brown shirt and pants turned black with grease and steel shavings who needed to track down some parts for a vehicle. He spoke no English but agreed to let me join him on the scavenger hunt. A car radiator sat on the backseat. I was nervous to leave Kris and Alex alone. No one spoke even a word of English.

We drove through this dog-eat-dog city for a couple of hours looking for parts, and I never once saw a person smile. Armed soldiers were everywhere, but they certainly didn't make one feel safe.

There were no real buildings where we went, just mile upon mile of wooden shacks, stained with old grease, stacked on smelly dirt. They were full of odds and ends, but none carried what we needed. The humid air stunk like diesel fumes and old sweat, and burning trash created a constant haze in the air. The smell reminded me of Gurugu, stinging my eyes and conjuring my ghosts. I thought back to my refugee friends and their unresolved struggles.

Back at the orphanage where we were finishing repairs on our bikes, the children were just starving for affection. As we worked, a boy maybe two years old—wearing a pink rag with elastic around the waist that revealed most of his crotch—came by, begging to be held, touched, looked at, talked to, anything to show that he was the object of our attention. He would not stop touching me. Twenty other little boys all wanted the same. I couldn't wait until I had a wife and could take kids like this home and give them a family.

We ended up spending about two weeks in Burundi with Dan and Tambry and helped out at the orphanage as we could. We treated our hosts to a couple dinners—anything to give them a break. Their load was overwhelming and they didn't get many visitors. At one point they took us down to the Rusizi River that flows into Lake Tanganyika. This place was world renowned for man-eating crocodiles and families of hippos. An armed guard was waiting at the turnoff, ready to charge us a small fee for entering Burundi's national park. We paid, and he hopped in the back of the truck with us, wanting to see the hippos himself. Dan found a whole herd of hippos about eighty yards out in the river, floating lazily in the water.

Austin whipped out his wrist rocket and looked for rocks. The guard put two and two together and hopped out of the truck, but instead of reprimanding the boy for trying to shoot stones at the hippos, he immediately started looking for stones himself. Austin slung a few rocks, but wasn't strong enough to land any in the herd. I gave it a shot. I could get the rocks far enough, but for the life of me couldn't hit any hippos. Alex took the slingshot and lobbed his first shot way up into the air over the hippos. It came down right on a big fat hippo's head, and they all at once started grunting and running through the river. We all cheered. The park ranger was thrilled.

"Nice shot, kid," I said to my brother. He always seemed to have a knack for things like this.

As our stay in Bujumbura ended, Dan and I discussed what roads were passable and where our next destination should be. We had been thinking about traveling east to the Serengeti, but another option serendipitously presented itself. The Democratic Republic of the Congo (DRC) government had in recent weeks signed a treaty with all of the different rebel factions. The treaty was unstable and not likely to last, but for the moment the guns were silent along a two-hundred mile stretch of untraveled road that connects the Congolese cities of Bukavu and Goma. Dan had contacts who we could stay with in each city. At the end of the road stood a huge active volcano that only a handful of intrepid travelers had ever climbed. Dan said we could see right into its fiery core on a clear day.

Every travel advisory we could get said we'd never be able to get into the DRC; they told us there wasn't even a government to request visas from. "Even if you could get in," they said, "it's not a place you would want to be." They didn't know us very well.

Actually, they didn't know Africa very well either. I don't blame them; so much in Africa is just hearsay. You have to really dig to get reliable information.

Dan, on the other hand, knew the situation, and he knew us. "You can make it," he said.

Good enough. We would head into utter chaos guaranteed to make Burundi look tame—the first white men to travel this road in over a decade according to the locals.

The narrow road through DRC offered a spectacular view of Lake Kivu, but the precarious "passing lane" to the right of the road demanded attention.

MOBBED

Eastern Democratic Republic of Congo

⌖

We left the relative stability of Bujumbura by 8 a.m. and already felt the heat. Soldiers weighed down with extra clips and grenades were conspicuously positioned every two hundred yards along the road, their barrels trained on us. Some cheered as we passed; most just glared at us with bloodshot eyes.

We entered Congo. I knew we had moved beyond any place sane people would even think about visiting. Exceptionally bold tourists could find safaris that offered them the chance to see Tanzania's Katavi National Park but that stop marked the end of the tourist's road, and we had passed it a long ways back. As we got through the border, several NGO workers with armored escorts proceeded by. No one we met could believe what we were doing—or what we had already done. They all talked to us like we were out of our minds. I hoped they were wrong.

A small bribe got us through the border. Never mind the paperwork.

Most of the foreign relief workers we bumped into in this region seemed to be at one extreme or the other. Either they were totally ignorant of how dangerous this place was and existed in a perpetual state of good-willed denial or they were so shell-shocked they could barely function. Maybe the difference was just a matter of time.

I was nervous. Kris and Alex didn't seem to be. I was nervous because I felt responsible. As usual it was my idea to come through eastern DRC. Of course Alex and Kris had been equally excited about the opportunity, but now I was questioning whether this was such a great plan. The open and still very active war had slowed down, but troops, militias, and rebels were armed, on patrol, and receiving no food or pay. They wandered through the jungle villages raping women and children and pillaging whatever supplies they found of interest. The city of Goma just outside the Rwandan border was at least an eight-hour drive from Bukavu if all went well. It had been four weeks since the last battle on that road. We just needed one day.

Please, just one day.

The military checkpoints along the way could be problematic, but we had lots of bribe money. The locals were desperate and poor, but our bikes were fast if things were to heat up.

We had been getting pounded by rain all day and were wet to the core by the time we arrived at our first stop, Bukavu, where a missionary family that Dan knew had been living and working since 1928. They were excited to have visitors and warmly welcomed us into their home. Their gate closed behind us, and I could breathe again. A little oasis, a home with a family. If I didn't know better, I might have thought Congo was a happy place.

The light drained from the sky, the city quieted down. The sun rose, the commotion started all over.

Kris was sick, probably giardia, an intestinal parasite. He slept most of the day while Alex took it easy. I decided to venture out into Bukavu, hoping to restock our tools. We had lost or broken a lot since leaving South Africa almost three thousand miles earlier and tomorrow's road to Goma was not a time to be ill-prepared.

Life was slower here. I took three hours to walk through muddy stone streets, picking through rusty toolboxes, exercising my best French. The city was a dump. I sifted through old scavenged tools trying to piece together a kit that would get us through. The rain meant a slippery day's travel was likely.

War's ugly face showed itself everywhere I looked—bombed buildings, armed men in uniform. UN peacekeepers offered me confused waves from the back of armored personnel carriers. They were in full armor, locked and loaded and on high alert. I walked with nothing.

As best I could tell, the people didn't operate by any recognized law or set of standards. I got the feeling that should someone choose to shoot and kill me for no apparent reason, very little if any consequences would follow.

The view here, however, was beautiful. Jagged green mountains next door to a beautiful blue lake. It looked like the perfect place to swim, but even the lake, home to a host of diseases and parasites, was deadly.

I had been gone long enough and had found enough tools. I got on my walkie-talkie and called Alex. He was on the other end of the city, cautiously exploring. We were both ready to head back to the house.

Kris was still in bed but said he'd be good for tomorrow's journey. It promised to be an intense stretch, especially with rumors of rebel activity along the road.

+

We left Bukavu early. At the edge of the city we heard a bloodcurdling scream that was straight out of hell. Just off the road was a three-hundred-pound swine on its back with a steel rod stuck in its throat. The scream turned into more of a gurgle as the beast began to drown in its own blood. Alex looked back at me with uneasy eyes. That sight and sound, that one moment, perfectly captured the mood of this ominous country.

Otherwise the day began without incident. Smooth military checkpoints, good road, fantastic scenery, people in dugout canoes fishing in the lake. We were beginning to think that the rest of the trip to Goma would go a lot easier than we had anticipated. We should have known better. We still had one hundred and forty miles of one-lane, two-way dirt and rock road through and over mountain passes.

We descended two thousand feet with nothing but a vertical drop into the blue on the right side of the road. Maniac drivers came whipping around blind corners, completely unyielding to foreigners on dirt bikes. We had been riding for about four hours when it happened.

Kris was in the lead, I was next, and Alex was bringing up the rear. We went flying around a left curve heading slightly uphill just as a van with about a dozen passengers came barreling down in the opposite direction, right in the middle of the road. Kris swerved right to the outside of the curve, barely avoiding a head-on collision. If he had gone much farther, he would have found himself in the lake four hundred feet below. I had more time and easily got out of the way. We both stopped and waited for Alex, listening for a collision.

A man alongside the road motioned to us that something was wrong. My heart dropped through the soles of my boots, and we both ripped back down the road.

Alex had been trying to catch up to us when he approached the curve. He looked up and the van was directly in front of him, not leaving much room on either side of the road. With an instant to think, Alex saw he couldn't swerve to the right because he would have flown off the side of the mountain, so he pushed hard left. The van nailed him.

Alex didn't remember exactly how it all happened, but the front right corner of the van clipped his handlebars. The bike smashed into the side of the van and Alex's arm went into the open side window, sending him flying through the air. Somehow he ended up on his feet standing next to his bike, which was pretty banged up but amazingly still running. The whole side of the van was smashed with a big red and black streak down the middle of its once solid-white door. Alex must have been going 35 mph when they hit. The van had to be traveling at least that.

Dismounting our bikes, Kris and I approached just as the mostly angry Congolese passengers had gathered around. I ran to Alex, Kris to the bike. An old local was inspecting Alex's hand by pushing and pulling everywhere one might expect to find a broken bone. I nudged the old man aside and grabbed Alex, inspecting him myself. Certainly something was injured.

He seemed as surprised as me by his response. "I think I'm okay, just a little shook up. I'll be fine."

I couldn't believe it. He couldn't be okay. Not even one broken bone? How could it be?

Kris stood the bike up. By looking at the damage on the van you would have never believed that the dirt bike—still in one piece, still running—caused that damage. We knew our bikes were tough, but we didn't expect them to go head to head with a van and win.

The number of bystanders had multiplied. Kris jumped on the bike to evaluate the damage.

An angry man tried to grab the keys from the ignition and shouted, *"Donnez-moi les clés. Vous paierez pour cela!"*

Kris yelled for the man to get back. The man looked like he was about to swing a fist at my friend. I shoved the man back into twenty others who were all clearly sided against us and growing increasingly hostile. Kris wisely let him take the keys. A fight was coming; we were ready, but not hopeful.

"Kris, get Alex," I shouted, "and get out of here!"

I smiled disarmingly at the irate driver and put my open hands into the air.

The driver of the van was hysterical. *"Vous devez payer! Donnez-nous de l'argent pour cela! Donnez-nous de l'argent ou vous ne partirez pas!"* He was insisting that we pay for the damages to his vehicle.

Behind him was a crowd of people that had been enduring war for years. They had suffered, and now an opportunity to get something free from the rich white men presented itself. All of them began screaming at me at once, demanding money.

I waved my arms, trying to draw the crowd's attention away from Alex and to give Kris a chance to get our bikes prepped to ride again. We would probably need to be able to run, and Alex's bike needed a lot of love before we could do that.

"Pas probleme. Ne pas probleme," I coaxed.

The driver again demanded money.

"Je ne pas probleme. Come, come. *Je argent."*

The crowd skeptically followed me down the hill some paces—away from the bikes, away from my brother.

"There is no problem," I said in a language I hardly knew, attempting to exude an air of authority. "I have all of the money. We will pay for all of the damages."

The driver resumed yelling; he wanted $100 for the damages to his van. All I had was $300 in my waist strap. I couldn't show them that. It would start a feeding frenzy.

"Cent dollars sont trop," I bargained, hoping to buy some time. Too much money, I said. And it was.

The crowd returned their attention to the bikes for a moment, just long enough for me to get the money out of my waist strap and into different pockets. I placed a fifty in my right pocket, two twenties in my left, and two one hundred dollar bills in my cargo pocket. Whatever I ended up giving them I wanted them to think it was all I had. Unfortunately, they had also begun to walk back toward Kris and Alex.

"Hey, hey, okay! *Pas probleme. Venez ici. Nous parler,"* I shouted.

Again they turned in my direction. The driver was still holding our keys. He felt in control, thinking we couldn't go anywhere as long as he had them. Little did he know Alex and Kris already had a spare key in each ignition.

Alex had been helping Kris, but now he was coming to make sure that I was okay.

"Hey, you turn around, get on the good bike and get out of here!" I screamed at him. "Go two miles up the road and wait, but get out of here now!" Getting my brother out of the situation was my biggest concern, but of course he refused to leave me in this uncertainty. Instead he indicated that the bikes were good to go; we could make a run for it if we needed to. Of course the mob separated me from our getaway. I offered the driver $20 for the damages, hoping he would think that we didn't have any more than that. No deal. He freaked out. The mob became even more restless.

Kris was at my bike, and thirty or forty people were surrounding him, unzipping our bags and grabbing at our gear.

Alex was another forty yards away with a comparable group around him. Why wouldn't he just start that bike and get away? I kept attempting to negotiate. By this time a couple of other vehicles had been stopped by the mob, now over a hundred people in size.

Just then a rebel soldier wearing a ripped and faded set of camouflage fatigues angrily stomped his way into our midst. As he did, people fell silent. A worn AK-47 with a big fat banana magazine hanging out of it was slung loosely over his shoulder. He had someplace he needed to be and was clearly angry that he couldn't get through.

The van driver explained the situation and begged the soldier to help get $100 for the damages. Other spectators echoed that they too were entitled to some compensation.

The rebel said that he was going to keep $10 for himself; they could have whatever was left. Everyone was silent now. They wouldn't question anything the soldier said. He looked into me with dead eyes. His presence didn't do anything to help remedy the situation, and he didn't care about resolving the problem. He was just one more person looking to profit. Of course, he had a loaded AK-47, had killed before, and would willingly do so again; clearly his say in this situation was absolute. Now instead of dealing with an angry mob I had to deal with one angry soldier. If he was happy, no one else mattered. As long as he was there, the mob was kept at bay.

The gunman told me to come. He grabbed his AK and pointed it at the side of the van and then at me.

"Cinquante dollars pour ce dommage."

The driver began to contest, but it was clear the soldier was not in the mood to play games.

"Pas probleme; d'accord," I said, and pulled out the fifty-dollar bill, exposing the empty pocket to the untrusting driver. The soldier reached for it, and I pointed to the keys. The driver slowly handed them over. We made the exchange all at once.

"Merci; au revoir," and I turned around to go. I signaled to Kris that we had to leave. NOW!

He was only twenty yards from me with our stuff, set to fly. My bike was further up the road, but not more than forty yards away. The mob, realizing that their opportunity to profit more significantly from our misfortune was about to drive away, began shouting, *"L'arrêt! Attend! Ne partez pas! Il y a un probleme!"*

I heard them behind me but never even looked back. I had the keys and the deal had been made. Three more vehicles full of people had stopped by now. They all started following, trying to stop me. I walked as quickly as I could, knowing that as soon as I started to run they would sprint. Kris was behind me now on his bike. The crowd wrapped around him and grabbed him. He opened the throttle and burst through them. I got to the crashed bike. Alex was sitting on my bike twenty yards further up on the road, just staring at me with worried eyes. Two people were about to reach him.

"ALEX, GET OUT OF HERE!"

They were all grabbing at me as I threw my leg over my bike and started it. I was waiting for a club to come down on my head. As soon as the engine turned over, I opened the throttle and plowed through the crowd. Just then Alex took off. One of the vans took off behind us, trying to catch us. They hadn't given up yet. But we were on three 650cc dirt bikes—they were hardly a match.

After a dozen more checkpoints, patrolled by at least three different rebel factions, and several more bribes, we reached the no-less-anarchic city of Goma.

Fifteen kilometers to its north loomed the volcano of Nyiragongo, glowing red and hurling smoke into the sky. But that was to be tomorrow's adventure. Today we were just happy to be alive.

Alex and the volcano. That speck on the summit to his left is me.

INTO THE FIRE

Eastern Democratic Republic of Congo

Talk about a shrinking planet. There in the middle of Africa, our next contact was Elli, an American-educated Haitian who worked for World Relief in Goma. This trip would have been impossible if we hadn't had people like Elli and others to hook up with at each stop along the way. He found us a nice place for dinner, surely the only one of its kind in Goma; we even ordered pizza.

The evening flew by as we recounted the day's ordeal to our new friend. I still couldn't believe the miracle that Alex was okay. The crash could have easily killed him. We were being looked after, that much was certain.

As night fell, we were treated to an even more spectacular view of Nyiragongo. Goma itself was nearly a mile above sea level and the completely freestanding volcano towered another six thousand feet over the city. It looked like something that belonged in a movie—a big round mountain with a crater at the top spewing sulfur gas into the sky. At this time of day the clouds hovering above the volcano glowed an eerie orange, making it almost appear as if the sun had set inside.

Just a couple of years ago Nyiragongo erupted, sending a huge river of lava right through Goma and into the nearby lake, destroying half the city. Dozens of homes and rusted cars partially buried in lava rock still covered a mile-wide stretch directly through the center of town.

We stayed the night at Elli's place. He had a small home behind a larger mansion. Before we went to sleep, he offered us a little bit of comfort: "If you hear gunshots coming from right outside the house, don't worry. The governor lives next door and they have lots of guns. Most of the bullets are going the other direction."

"Oh, good," I responded sarcastically.

Elli didn't pick up on it. He smiled and wished us good night.

+

Morning came far too soon. We were up around 7 a.m. To my continued amazement, Alex was able to walk.

"How you feelin', tough guy?"

"Me? I'm a little stiff. Nothing a couple ibuprofens won't fix."

We had to run some errands. The crash had shattered the rear braking mechanism on Alex's bike. We needed a bit of scrap metal, a welder, and some wrench time to make it usable again.

In the city, small groups of soldiers carrying grenades, RPGs, 50-cals, and AK-47s were omnipresent. I couldn't even keep track of what rebel faction they represented.

"You guys about ready for a climb?" Alex asked.

We had been hoping to climb the volcano, but after the crash Kris and I had given up on the idea. Alex couldn't possibly handle it after what he had just been through.

"Are you serious?" I asked.

"Yeah. It will be good for me to loosen up," he said.

"If you're sure you're up to it."

We didn't get to the base of the volcano until one that afternoon. Normally summitting was a two-day deal, but we were going to try to summit and return the same day. The paramilitary soldiers in the ranger house at the trailhead insisted that we hire a guide because apparently the last group to climb were robbed at gunpoint of absolutely everything they had and stumbled down from the frosty peak wearing just their underwear. We agreed to pay, and a soldier in worn-out fatigues with a loaded and cocked AK around his shoulder joined our trio.

The trail shot straight up the mountain without so much as one switchback. The first couple of hours we hiked on a narrow path through jungle rain forest; but for the remainder of the trek we traversed cooled lava rock, watching smoke rise from crevasses. We reached the summit in a quick but strenuous three hours.

The top was cold and lifeless; toxic gas had killed everything except short, scrubby bushes. At first we were lost in the clouds and could see nothing except the ground beneath our feet. Yet it was impossible to miss the roar of the volcano coming from a thousand feet within the crater. It sounded like the surf in the middle of a storm but with no pattern of repetition; chaos articulated with the occasional explosion of flammable gas.

Not long after our ascent, it started to pour. We had rain gear, but it was still cold, and we had no shelter. Fortunately, Alex used the ready supply of bushes to build and maintain a fire, which warmed us and our armed guard. When at last the rain stopped, the sun must have been getting close to the horizon. Twilit clouds flashed an amber hue all around us as lightning danced through the sky. Above us the thunder still rolled while below us the volcano hissed.

So this is what you look like.

Eventually the clouds blew over altogether, revealing a dark blue canopy overhead. The thunderstorm was off troubling some other mountain. "Do you think God kept you alive yesterday just so you could see his majesty today?" Kris asked Alex softly, breaking the silence.

But Alex wasn't there with us. He was dancing on the clouds, flying with the lightning, growling with the thunder. He was lost somewhere in the middle of the splendor that surrounded us. He was somewhere peaceful, somewhere happy, somewhere intimate.

"Somebody upstairs is looking out for us," Kris said. "Erik, coming on this trip was the best decision I've ever made."

"There's no one else I would have attempted this with."

Sunset was only thirty minutes away, yet we waited patiently; we wanted to see the lava in the dark before we descended. Meanwhile, below us we could see the entire city of Goma and a breathtaking view of Lake Kivu. The setting sun was such a sight that the lake couldn't help but hold up a mirror to share the splendor.

Thank you, God.

The wind cleared the smoke out of the crater, exposing the volcano's red-hot core. It was a straight drop from the rim with the exception of a few layers where lava had recently risen. We could see right down into the molten lava, churning and exploding fifty feet in the air. It was like a little window from the highest heaven into the fires of hell. We sat mesmerized, staring into the pit, unable to move. As darkness took hold around us, the whole inside of the crater was illuminated in scarlet, the emerging cloud resembling a perpetual sunset.

This was one of the greatest moments I had ever known, and I was sharing it with my only brother and the best friend a man could ever hope for. This was the life I was meant to live. I was right where I was supposed to be, I had never been so sure.

Long after the sun had gone to sleep, we started our descent. The sky behind us was painted maroon. We stopped only once on the way down to sit in awe on the cooled lava flow and to stare at the myriad stars. It was dark, it was silent, it was still. For an hour we sat motionless.

Finally Kris whispered, "Are you ready?"

Alex and I shouldered our packs and without a word we continued the descent. We were nearly at the bottom when our guide heard voices ahead and motioned for us to kill the lights and get down. His finger massaged the trigger of his rifle as he probed the blackness ahead. The voices yelled something in a language we couldn't understand; the soldier eased. A couple of minutes later we came upon some of his fellow soldiers on the trail.

We descended in record time. The men at the base camp seemed surprised that we were still so cheerful after the hike. Elli was also waiting for us. We were ready to eat and get some sleep, but still needed to make it safely through a few military checkpoints before we could enjoy those luxuries.

Bidding thanks and farewell to our gracious host, we packed up the next day and braved the border into Rwanda. Borders were never fun, but this one was particularly bad. After several hours of coaxing and a few small bribes, the Congolese border patrol finally let us pass and we entered the now stable country of Rwanda. It was only a short drive on paved roads to the country's capital, Kigali. There another World Relief worker was expecting us—we hoped.

HOPE FOR TOMORROW

Rwanda

Two brothers trying in vain to take in the beauty. Could life be any better?

It was just eleven years ago that men marched down this very road and every other in Rwanda with machetes, slaughtering all who shared the name Tutsi—men, women, and children. No one was spared. In the three months the genocide lasted, over eight hundred thousand innocent people were murdered.

Today the highways and streets of Rwanda were freshly paved. New buildings were being built. New life was being born and new hope was taking form.

Alex was in front. Kris was riding fifty yards behind me. The smooth black asphalt was a refreshing change of pace—the first good road since South Africa, the first paved road since Zambia.

A smiling woman wearing a brightly-colored orange, black, and red piece of fabric led a flock of sheep down the road. She waved to us as we passed. Crops filled every valley, and animals grazed on every hillside. Around every corner was another breathtaking view. Mountains with hollowed out tops lay dormant, like ancient dragons watching over the land. A vivid emerald landscape blanketed the fertile black soil.

My bike hummed. The wind sang. The air was clean. It took a couple of hours to reach Kigali. By now we needed gas. As soon as our bikes stopped moving, sixty Rwandans had completely encircled us at the pump and were harmlessly staring. Here we could get around in English, but the primary language spoken among the locals was still Swahili.

"Mzungu, eh, mzungu," was all they said to us.

I called our contact, P.J. He was coming to meet us.

Dan in Burundi had told him about our motorcycle trip and about our braving the infamous road through DRC. Apparently P.J. himself was a rider. He was excited to hear about our journey north thus far; we were excited to relive the experience.

After a hot shower we went out for dinner, P.J.'s treat. We were starving. Two of his Rwandan friends, who were about my age, joined us. I had so many questions for them. They had just as many for us. We feasted on fish and umgali, a white substance comparable to grits that was the main staple in much of Africa. After the meal Alex went into the back of P.J.'s van and fell asleep. I think the crash had taken more of a toll on him than he realized. Kris was struggling to stay conscious as I chattered away.

Neither of the Rwandan men had been present during the genocide, but both had lost family. I had the distinct honor of talking with them about the future of Rwanda and how they felt about the government's handling of current problems. The youth, they said, were ready to go forward; justice must be and was being carried out in the local tribunals; but the focus was on tomorrow. The genocide was like a scar on Rwanda's face, but people were learning from it and they were determined to never let it happen again. Rwanda was ready to forgive and move on.

I couldn't believe that these people were capable of living peaceably beside those who had committed such horrendous acts. Yet they were, and as a result Rwanda was painting a beautiful tomorrow. I was amazed.

We stayed only one night in Rwanda before pressing on toward Kenya via Uganda. The road was paved and travel relatively calm, with only one major exception when a near brush with a semitruck sent Kris barreling over his handlebars going fifty miles per hour. He walked away from the crash with nothing but a scraped-up helmet and riding jacket, but his bike demanded special attention before it was roadworthy again.

After three days of hard riding, some time on the side of the road with wire and wrenches, and two more international borders, we reached the bustling metropolis of Nairobi, the first city with fast food and a movie theater in over five thousand miles of biking. Mike was scheduled to meet us there in just two more days.

Welcome to Africa, Mike. Mike (left) and Kris.

WHAT'S THE SCORE?

Nairobi, Kenya

Civilization was intimidating. Neatly dressed people drove nice clean cars through busy streets. It had been a long time since we had seen tall buildings or stoplights. We felt out of place here.

Mike's service in the Air Force ended two days prior. Tomorrow evening he was scheduled to fly into the Nairobi airport. Our band of brothers would be complete. We would finish this adventure together.

Because he hadn't been able to jump through the hoops of getting a dirt bike and shipping it to Africa, Mike first thought he might not be able to join us. But Alex, Kris, and I would hear none of that nonsense. As if we couldn't adjust to a change of plans.

"Don't worry about it, Mike," we told him. "You can ride on the back of one of our bikes the last four thousand miles to Egypt. We'll ship everything that we don't absolutely need back to the States to lighten our load and throw you on the back for the rest of the trip. They are two-person bikes, you know."

We weren't about to give up the companionship of our friend just because of some silly little logistical issue like no vehicle. Speaking of which, our own bikes once again needed some tender loving care. Our shocks were basically blown. Alex's front rim was terribly bent. We needed oil changes. We needed new plugs. The parts Mike was bringing with him and the tools I scavenged up in DRC should do the trick. In a couple of days the bikes would be as good as new.

Our contact in Nairobi was a schoolteacher named Carrie. We stopped at a gas station so I could give her a call and get directions to her house. She lived on the grassy, tree-filled campus where she taught. Just as our other hosts had, she welcomed us graciously. A hot shower and a carpeted floor were awaiting us. Modern life! We were all due for a cleaning. The water hit my face and ran down my dark body, turning the bottom of the shower brown. Afterward, my skin was a few shades lighter. I had been thinking I was just really tan. The dust dislodged from the cracks of my eyes and roots of my hair. My skin could breathe again. Now I was ready for a nap.

The first day we just rested. We lay in the shade, ate ourselves into a stupor, and lounged on the soft floor.

The sun set. Alex was already fast asleep.

"I can't wait for Mike to get here," Kris whispered.

"It's going to be fun, all of us together trying to figure out the rest of this continent."

The city was quiet.

"Tomorrow we'll have to go to the Sudanese embassy and pick up our visas."

"We'll swing by the Ethiopian and Egyptian embassies too. Make sure everything is in order," I added.

"Everything should be all set."

We both laughed.

"Hey," he said after a long pause, "did you hear Carrie mention that there was a volleyball court somewhere up at the school?"

"Me and Alex versus you and Mike?"

"You're going down."

"We'll see about that."

✦

"Sorry," the Sudanese official at the embassy said unconvincingly from across the table. "Americans cannot enter without a special invitation from the Sudanese government."

"So you mean to tell me that in the last two and a half months that we have been in the jungle, Sudan has completely changed their border policy?"

She stared indifferently at me. I think she only understood about half of what I said.

"Call the embassy in South Africa," I urged. "They already approved our visas. We just needed to pick them up here."

"We can't call them. Our embassies don't have long-distance service. We don't know when the policy will change again. You can wait if you want. This all happened about a month ago. NEXT."

"Hey, excuse me!" I said, not about to give up so easily. "There has to be some way we could get into Sudan."

"No, no way. NEXT PERSON."

Alex and Kris had gone to the Ethiopian and Egyptian embassies this morning. I was at the Sudanese embassy alone. They were not going to be happy about this change of plans. After a quick bite to eat I got on the Internet. Someone I knew had to know a way into Sudan. I met the guys back at Carrie's house an hour later.

"How did things go at Ethiopia and Egypt?"

"Good. We could buy visas here, but they said it would be cheaper just to buy them at the borders. We're good to go. How was Sudan?"

"Apparently a month ago, while we were somewhere in the jungle, they reformed their border policy. Our visas never got sent to this embassy and they are no longer approving Americans for visas at embassies outside of the US."

"Huh, you don't say. So what do we do?"

"I haven't given up yet, but it's not looking good. If worse comes to worse we can drive up into northern Ethiopia and then take a boat or a plane over Sudan."

"That might be what we'll have to do."

"When does Mike's flight get in?"

"In a few hours. Carrie said we could borrow her car to pick him up."

For the next few days I argued with the Sudanese embassy officials. I spent hours in the American embassy. I exhausted every contact I had and still got nowhere. We would have to bypass this one country and take a flight over the thousand-mile stretch of hot, sandy Sudan.

Mike arrived on schedule with a suitcase full of parts and a couple changes of clothes. We informed him of the new plans. He didn't much care. He was just stoked to be sharing this adventure with us. We were thrilled to finally have him.

We worked on the bikes, changing out old parts, tightening up loose bolts, refreshing the fluids. Dust caked every crack and crevice. Our poor bikes were tired. I think they were glad we weren't going to be traveling through Sudan.

A week later, our team was ready, our bikes were looking as good as they were going to, and the road was calling. It was evening; tomorrow morning we would roll—four guys, three bikes, and little else. But we were not going anywhere before a game of volleyball.

The court was in a large gymnasium. We had the place all to ourselves. Mike had had a beach court in his backyard when we were in high school. He, Kris, and I used to play all the time. Alex was an athletic kid, but he was smaller than the rest of us and would probably have chosen soccer over volleyball.

The game began. Mike served it to Alex. He tried to bump it over the net, but the ball went out of bounds.

One serving zero.

Mike sent it to me. I lateraled to Alex. He tried to set me for a spike, but the ball was too close to the net. Kris answered.

Two serving zero.

"Sorry, Erik."

"It's all good, bro."

The ball came whipping over the net. Alex got a hand on it. It was just high enough for me to get under it. "Here comes a set, Alex!"

I sent it over to Alex's side of the court, just off the net. He ran, jumped, and spiked the ball ... right into the net. Kris and Mike exchanged high fives. I could tell Alex was getting frustrated.

"Erik, just get it over the net."

Three serving zero.

Mike served strong, but it dropped short into the net. Now it was our turn. I took first serve.

It went over the net. Kris bumped it to Mike and then got ready to spike it. Alex ran up to the net for a block, but it got through. I was able to dig it. Alex got a hand on it, and it was back over the net.

"I'll get on the net, Alex. Get ready to return anything that gets past me."

But they tipped it over me just shy of Alex. It was Kris's turn to serve, four serving zero.

A few minutes later, now down seven to zero, Alex hollered, "Time out!

"Erik, you can score. Why do you keep sending it to me?"

"Alex, you're so close. If you couldn't do this I would quit setting you up, but it's right there. You can smash that ball. I'm going to set it right here. When you jump to hit it, don't close your fist. Open your hand and snap your wrist. You got this."

"Okay, we'll try it again but if you can score a point, just do it already. I don't want to get smoked fifteen to nothing."

"Hey, you guys ready?" Mike yelled.

"Yeah, go," Alex answered.

The ball floated over the net right to Alex. This was it. He sent it over to me and looked to the spot we just talked about.

"Here it comes, Alex!"

I set the ball. He ran up, jumped, and connected. Kris was on the net but couldn't get a hand on it. It was going too fast for Mike to reach. All eyes were fixed on the shot as it landed on the back corner endline.

Alex let out a triumphant shout. "THAT'S WHAT I'M TALKING ABOUT!" His face lit up.

Now it was his turn to serve. Zero serving seven.

Alex served it underhand over the net. Mike and Kris easily returned it. Alex got a hand on it. He passed it over to me.

"Set me, Erik!"

"Here you go."

He was already running forward, about to jump before I even got to touch the ball. I connected. It floated up to the spot.

SLAM.

Attaboy, Alex.

One serving seven.

Two serving seven.

Three serving seven.

"That's how it's done, Alex."

Four serving seven.

Now we were playing.

Mike and Kris ended up winning that game and the two that followed, but it didn't matter. Alex relived every play all the way back to the house and while the rest of us were trying to get to sleep. He was our team's leading scorer and had developed a wicked spike. When he got ahold of the ball no one could stop him.

I went to sleep with a smile on my face. I couldn't be happier.

Thank you.

DIVIDE AND CONQUER

Northern Kenya

Mike (left) and Alex taking a break just outside bandit territory.

Leaving Nairobi felt great. It was a beautiful city, but we had been there a week and it was time to move on. Our course was due north toward Ethiopia. Though it was sunny for the moment, in the distance we could see thunderstorms roll across the savanna in little patches that dropped sheets of water. Able to dodge a few storms, we eventually got dumped on. The rest of the drive was a chilly one. We didn't reach the day's destination, Isiolo, until long after dark.

The tarmac ended in Isiolo, and we were back on rocky dirt roads. Only one road headed through northern Kenya, so finding our way would not be a problem; surviving the one road might be. The Kenyans painted a negative picture of Ethiopia for us: "A dry nasty place full of corruption—why would you want to go there?"

The road between Isiolo and Ethiopia was very dangerous for a couple reasons. First, it wandered through hundred-mile stretches of extreme dry heat with no water, shade, refuge, or relief whatsoever. The only way in or out was the worn, rutty, rocky, dirt road. If something broke you either had to fix it or leave it. Second, if you couldn't get yourself out, help was unlikely; traffic seldom braved the road because bandits and militias occupied the unpatrolled vast expanses of northern Kenya and attacks on travelers were common. Those who had to travel north from Isiolo went in convoys and were often accompanied by a military escort.

We started out at 8 a.m. and immediately realized that we had a problem. Riding with Mike on the back of Kris's bike was uncomfortable on the pavement, but manageable. On this road, however, it was absolutely torturous. Every bump, every rock, every rut we ripped over sent a shock wave right through the passenger's back. Multiply that by hundreds every few seconds. It was almost unbearable.

Mike endured 30 km of the abuse before he could take no more. With 500 km remaining before we hit our next stretch of tarmac—and reports that the road between only got worse, including 160 km of barren desert—our situation looked grim. I offered to trade spots with Mike. Let him drive my bike and spread the burden out a bit. In less than 15 km I was done. This was not going to work.

Up ahead we noticed a cloud of dust hanging over the road, apparently a convoy that hadn't stopped in Isiolo. It didn't take long to catch them. Four heavy trucks were traveling from Nairobi to the northernmost city in Kenya, Moyale, the trailers loaded with cargo and rubberized covers stretched over the tops. Several men were perched on one of the covers watching us drive by.

I yelled to Kris, "Pull in front of the last truck."

I motioned to the driver that I wanted to climb up top and ride with them. He nodded his head, and seconds later I had hopped off Kris's idling bike and climbed the truck's ladder to the trailer. Of the four riders, one was wearing silver Adidas sunglasses, a black bandana, a big silver chain, jeans, and a yellow and green flannel shirt. He greeted me and proudly lit a cigarette with a worn box of stick matches. The other three men just looked at me.

A small, cramped space at the front of the trailer seemed to be reserved for the passengers. The bottom was full of sacks of potatoes, but sitting on them were four Massi men, decorated with bead necklaces, bracelets, and anklets, their earlobes stretched as was their custom. Skinny yet strong looking, they each had just a walking stick with them. They barely acknowledged my presence and continued their conversation by clicking incomprehensible sounds at each other.

Riding in convoy seemed perfect: we had the cover of the big metal trucks if the Bantus started taking their pot shots; we were protected from the bandits, from the unforgiving terrain. Ideally Alex, Mike, and Kris would ride alongside the trucks for the next couple hundred kilometers until the next stop. But that wasn't an option. It was like the old story of the tortoise and the hare: the motorcycles were fast—we could cover three times more ground than a convoy of trucks—but we couldn't maintain that rate for more than a couple hours at a time. We needed to stop and rest. The trucks on the other hand would press forward slowly—one kilometer after another after another—without stopping until they reached their destination. If my crew stayed with the convoy, they would be too exhausted after the first hundred kilometers to finish the day's journey. They needed to go on ahead.

The truck had started up again. I signaled to Kris that all was well by putting my thumb in the air. He returned the gesture and yelled, "See you at the next stop." Wherever that might be.

Alex and Mike were stopped a couple hundred meters up the road and were waiting for Kris to catch up. They each gave a thumb's up and took off in a burst.

I was on my own now.

The ride on top of the truck was hot and uncomfortable, but it did give me a chance to look around — something you could do little of while maneuvering a motorcycle on challenging terrain. Huge herds of camels, hundreds of them, roamed through the brush. We passed several villages of other tribes, cousins to the Massi. The men all wore decorative beads. They had long threads woven into their hair that extended halfway down their backs and were dusted red with a particular type of soil found in the bush. They each carried with them a small sword and a spear to protect themselves from the lions and cheetahs that lived in this region. The women tending cattle were naked except for the bright red fabric wrapped around their waist and a colorful collection of beads around their necks.

The terrain had completely changed from lovely grassland to savanna to sun-scorched brush with rugged mountains jutting out from the ground. Everything was brown, though every so often a vibrant purple flower bush would burst through the monotonous landscape or a speck of red would appear in the distance — a tribesman armed with his spear observing the convoy.

The convoy stopped occasionally to repair a flat tire. Whenever we did, the driver and his minions harassed me for money.

"I have nothing. You saw me get aboard. When we reach our destination I will be able to pay you in full."

I found a spot on top of the truck and tried to make myself comfortable. Every hole in the ground sent the top of the truck whipping from one side to the other. Falling asleep was out of the question; I would wake up on the side of the road as soon as the truck hit the first bump—and there were plenty of bumps. I lay back and looked at the blue sky.

The sun was just a few inches over the horizon, but already I could feel its heat. It was going to be a hot one.

In the midst of all the adventure, in the center of the uncertainty, long stretches of quiet comforted me. I could do nothing but be. My thoughts and prayers were the only company I had.

I needed no distractions.

I longed for nothing.

I sat and I was.

I was free.

+

The land got drier every hour that passed. For the first six hours of the ride no one said a thing to me, nor I to them. I sat content observing, thinking, wondering, admiring. The long stretches of silence didn't bother me anymore, and to be honest I didn't want to reveal any more than necessary to people I didn't know. They had no idea who I was or what I was doing there. The obscurity gave me a sense of security.

Many of the men riding in the convoy were chewing on *qat*, a drug that gives its users a euphoric high that lasts the better part of the day but leaves them extremely depressed and irritable for just as long when they come back down. Right now they were all dancing around on top of the trucks. It was only a matter of time before the other side of the coin showed its face.

One of my trailer mates had been watching me ever since I climbed aboard. At first I didn't even notice him. He was quiet and reserved, not at all threatening. Over time he moved closer and closer—he was sitting right next to me now—but I still paid him no attention.

"My name in Josephates. I am returning home after visiting my mother in Nairobi."

In Western culture people often wear their lives on their sleeves. It isn't uncommon to reveal a lot of personal information about family or a job in a casual conversation with a recent acquaintance. But in Africa information is power and it is often guarded. This guy wasn't just chatting to pass the time, he was extending an invitation to become his friend.

"Hello, I'm Erik. My friends and I are traveling to Ethiopia."

"Ethiopia? Why would you want to go there?"

I just laughed.

The two of us hit it off. As we bumped along the seemingly endless road toward Ethiopia, Josephates told me stories about the different tribes that lived in this region. He told me stories of the first white missionaries to come through a half century earlier, bringing the gospel to the people. Now almost everyone embraced some vague mix of Christianity and local spiritualism. We talked about the dangers of the bush and the needs of the people living in it. We lay side by side on the top of the truck and stared into the sky. Nine hours had passed since I first joined this motorized caravan. The sun was now a big red ball just inches off the horizon, illuminating our floating canvas with every shade of orange and red imaginable. We had endured its merciless heat all day; we had earned this sunset.

More bumps, more shakes. The light faded, the brilliant stars eased into their places. No rush. As Josephates and I stargazed, I told him the stories of Orion the mighty hunter, of his two dogs, and the timeless battle between Orion and Scorpio that replays itself every night. Finally he pointed to a speck of light in the distance. We were nearing Marsabit, the next and only stop before the desert that separates Ethiopia and Kenya. We both anxiously watched the lights grow closer.

When at last the truck stopped, taking only a short break before finishing its journey, the driver immediately demanded his money. The rest of the crew were starting to come off their high and were much less friendly than they had been earlier in the day. I was so tired and hungry that a night's rest and a good meal were all I could think about. I asked when the next convoy might be coming through.

"Tomorrow night, I think," answered someone.

If we didn't want to try to double up a bike for the next half of the trip, I would need to get back on the caravan right now. I needed to find the guys.

"Has anyone seen three white people?" I shouted to some bystanders.

"Dey in dat hotel." The man pointed.

I ran down the street and into the hotel. There they were, absolutely exhausted, wandering through the café area. It had been a long, hard day of riding. They were beat.

"You guys, we've got desert for the next 250 km or so and there will probably be no more convoys coming through until tomorrow night."

Mike was a man of few words. If he were the type to complain, he would tell me how tough the day was and how much he was dreading the next day's ride. But he didn't. He didn't need to. He just looked at me with fresh bruises up and down his arms. Both elbows were missing skin.

"I don't think we'll be able to make the road if we have two on a bike," I continued. "I need to get back on this convoy. They're leaving in a few minutes."

"How was the ride?" Mike asked me.

"Hot and painful."

"That sounds about right."

Kris and Mike grabbed all the bags and started loading them into the convoy. Kris paid the driver.

Alex was quiet. He was obviously not excited about the idea. Spending one day apart in such uncertain circumstances was bad enough, but this had to be done. I would take all the gear on the truck with me and they would each have a bike free of any load other than themselves, some tools, and water. The bikes would be much faster and more maneuverable tomorrow on the stretch notorious for the Bantu bandits. The guys hopefully would be able to open up the throttle and outrun any trouble that might come their way.

Alex joined me as I grabbed a quick bite to eat. Kris and Mike were still loading things into the truck.

Josephates found me. "Erik, we're leaving."

I shoved one last bite into my mouth.

Kris showed up next, out of breath. "You ready to go, E? The trucks are about to roll!"

I pulled him aside for a moment. "Kris, look after my little brother. Get him to Moyale."

"With my life," he said sincerely. "Now get out of here."

I started running to the line of trucks, the first of which had already left. Alex was right beside me.

"You guys be safe and GET TO MOYALE!"

"Don't worry about us; we'll see you tomorrow."

"Watch your back, Erik," Mike said.

We hated splitting up again but had no other option. We had no phones, no email, and the walkie-talkies were only good over short distances, not a hundred miles of brutal desert. The only thing we knew was that we were to meet in Moyale. If for some reason they didn't show, I would wait a few days and then go searching. This next leg of road would be the worst—just a path marked by piles of stacked stones every few hundred meters to keep one from getting lost in the barren wasteland.

I gave Alex one last hug. "You be careful," I told him. "Get to Moyale no matter what."

Without a word he told me the same. Several dubious characters, all high on qat, sat on top of the truck. Alex looked over my shoulder and saw them. I could see his concern, but this wasn't our first time journeying into dangerous lands, negotiating tense situations.

I turned and started running toward the truck, which had already started rolling away.

"Got your knife on you?" he called.

I nodded my head, grabbed the side of the truck, and climbed aboard. Josephates had a spot saved for me.

All through the restless night the trucks rolled on. For the first couple of hours Josephates and I sat up top and watched for the animals that came out only at night. I spotted what resembled a deer except it was not much bigger than a house cat. Josephates pointed out another one of the creatures. "They call it a dik-dik," he said.

It wasn't long before we stopped seeing animals. All the dry brush gradually disappeared too and we embarked into an ocean of rock and sand. I looked up and bid the stars good night, thanking them for their company. A couple men still chewing their precious qat leaves were perched at the front of the trailer.

"Are you going to sleep tonight?"

"This doesn't let us sleep." They lifted the branch full of leaves, inviting me to share some.

I declined and climbed down into the now unoccupied passenger hold, dropping onto a sack of potatoes. The truck was barreling along. Convoys were able to travel a lot faster at night because the tires were cool and wouldn't explode when they went over the rocks. It was nice to be going faster, but all the dust kicked up by our caravan seemed to find its way into the trailer. It was almost suffocating, but I needed to sleep and this was the only place on the truck that constant attention wasn't required. I tied my shirt around my face and tried in vain to rest.

The trucks stopped a couple of times that night, I think more than anything because the drivers needed a break. I could hear all the crew climb down and wander through the convoy. Some just lay down on the desert floor and slept; others, particularly the antagonistic qat chewers, caused trouble for the rest. Scuffles between them and whoever was unfortunate enough to become involved seemed endless. Not wanting to attract any undue attention to myself, I rarely left my spot in the trailer. I lay awake and waited, counting the hours until sunrise.

The night passed, morning came, and eventually we arrived in the lawless border town of Moyale—a place that was beyond the reach of Kenyan authority. Moyale was a stepping-stone, the last stop on a road that no one wanted to brave, leading to a border that no one wanted to cross.

The trucks squeaked to a halt in the middle of what appeared to be the only intersection in town. People came running up to unload the cargo or to take what they could without being noticed.

I no longer looked very different from the Africans on the trucks. Our faces and clothes had all turned the same shade of brown, our hair matted down with dust, our faces caked with the fine substance. Josephates yelled to me, “Don’t let anyone touch your bags!”

I jumped down from the truck and was immediately swarmed by people offering to help me carry my things or asking for a small donation. Josephates threw the bags down to me one at a time. I stacked them right in front of me and put my leg on them. A boy of about sixteen grabbed one and tried to walk away. I grabbed his arm and jerked him back. He dropped the bag and started to run. My reaction kept other “helpers” at bay long enough to get all three bags together on the ground. Josephates grabbed one, I took the other two, and we walked through the crowd to a guesthouse. Many followed us.

“I need one room and none of these people are welcome with me,” I told the man behind the counter who was negotiating both the room reservations and taking orders for the hotel’s modest restaurant.

The owner yelled something to the crowd in a language I couldn’t understand and then led me to my room on the second floor. Josephates came with me.

The room’s one window had no glass or screens and the brown wooden shutter was broken. The walls were painted an awful pink. I thanked Josephates for all of his help; he gave me directions to his shop and asked that I come say good-bye before I left Kenya.

After locking the bags in the room, I found the communal bathroom. The place reeked of feces. A small toilet was backed up, and the floor and walls were covered with urine. From the wall hung a small spigot that leaked cold water. At least I could bathe. I cleaned myself the best I could, washed my clothes. The heat of the day had already started, but it didn't matter. I had been on that truck for twenty-four hours without a break. I was clean, refreshed, and on a stationary mat in a secure enough place. Now it was a waiting game. If all went well on the road, it would be several hours before my brother and friends arrived.

Please take care of those guys.

I dozed off to sleep.

+

I had just awakened from my nap when I heard the unmistakable rumble approaching. Down the road they came rolling—Alex leading the way. I knew they would make it ahead of schedule.

I leaned out my window. They parked in the street just below.

"Keep a close eye, this place is sketchy," I shouted down to them over the growling bikes.

Good job, guys.

The guys got up early that morning, they told me, determined to get this stretch of road done with as soon as they could. With no weight on their bikes they were able to keep a healthy speed—which was good because they had to make Moyale before nightfall. Though the road was long and grueling, they sped through the desert, through the Bantus' land, paying no attention to the would-be bandits marauding in the middle of nowhere. Not confined to any one route, the whole desert was their road. After just six hours of travel and no major mishaps, they reached Moyale.

Mike's face was caked with dust. "We didn't want you to get too lonely chillin' here all by yourself." He started to laugh but stopped himself. It was painful for him to laugh too hard. He must have taken a few more spills.

"The bikes take a little getting used to, huh?"

"Let's just say I'm ready for tarmac," Mike said. Kris and Alex chuckled.

Man, I love these guys.

"Muhumid would be proud, Alex," I said.

He cracked a half smile. "Yeah, he would."

"Who's Muhumid?" Mike asked.

"He's a man who can't be done justice with words," Alex answered.

"He's the guy who taught Alex and me to breathe fire."

"Huh?"

"I'll tell you over lunch. I've ordered us some food."

We hauled everything that wasn't fastened to our bikes up to my room before we ate, right past the now somewhat hesitant group of "helpers" ready to take anything of value off our hands. We sat down in the guesthouse's "restaurant" at a brown table covered with uneaten tidbits from at least a dozen meals, surrounded by mismatched wooden chairs. The man behind the counter who I had checked in with a few hours earlier signaled that the food was on its way.

"Okay, so what's the story with the fire breathing?" Kris asked as soon as he sat down.

Alex started: "One evening in Morocco, Erik and I were picking up workers from the job sites. Muhumid—the site supervisor we told you about before—and a government-appointed driver were waiting beside the front-end loader after a long day of clearing fallen houses and preparing a new building site. Erik and I climbed the narrow two-track up to the site and unloaded thirty-liter barrels of smelly diesel. We always filled the front-end loader up in the evening so it would be ready to go in the morning. As we were siphoning fuel into the tractor, Muhumid casually took the end of the hose, the end spitting the nasty fuel into the tractor, and held it to his mouth. Erik and I both gasped and yelled for him to stop, but he just smiled and motioned for us to watch."

I continued: "It looked like he was drinking the fuel. I was sure our next stop would be the hospital. When this brute's thirst for diesel was quenched, he stood up, held out a lighter, and exhaled a huge fireball into the sky. All the bystanders looked pleased. They must have been waiting for this. It was amazing."

"It was the coolest thing I had ever seen!" said Alex. "So of course I asked him to do it again."

"Muhumid didn't understand the words, but it was clear that everyone there wanted a repeat of the spectacle. So he filled his mouth again and unleashed another huge burst of flame. At that point, Alex leaned over to me and said, 'He has to show us how to do that.'

"After the tractor was fueled we headed back home, ready to learn Muhumid's secret. He brought a small pitcher full of fuel up onto our flat roof. It was dark, we all had our shirts off, and there was a torch lit in the center of us as if we were about to undergo some ceremonial rite of passage. Muhumid demonstrated again."

"The roof lit up, and we could feel the heat on our faces," added Alex.

"When it was my turn," I said, "I nervously approached the torch, determined to learn this stomach-turning stunt. Muhumid handed me a cup and the torch. I wished there was something to be explained, anything to buy me a little more time before I burnt my face off, but it was simple: blow the fuel over the fire, and chemistry will take over from there. I took a deep breath, filled my mouth with the disgusting fuel, and spit it out over the flame."

"BOOM! Erik lights the roof with a huge fireball! I was standing with Muhumid as proud of my big brother as ever," beamed Alex.

"I tried again. BOOM! A bigger one! I was starting to get the hang of it. Refill. BOOM! I spit and spit, filled my mouth with water and spit some more. It tasted terrible. Diesel fuel, like a fine scotch, must be an acquired taste," I said.

"Then I stepped up to bat," recalled Alex. "I was nervous but no less determined. I filled my mouth and—"

"BOOM! He burped a huge fireball on his first try!" I interrupted him again. "'Attaboy, little brother, attaboy,' as another fireball lit the roof. Muhumid was so proud. He said most people didn't want to learn this art. I didn't know if that was necessarily a compliment, but it did confirm the notion that had been bouncing around in my head for weeks. We were all the same breed, Alex, Muhumid, and I. We were from different worlds, but we were cut from the same fabric."

"He sounds like our kinda guy," said Kris.

"You would have loved him," answered Alex. "He regularly spent weeks at a time living off the land, wandering through the mountains. He knew what plants could be eaten, where he could get water, and how to start a fire. He hiked with just a small backpack, a hatchet, and a large knife. And he loved hunting wild African boar, these vicious beasts that can grow to over three hundred and fifty pounds and five feet long, armed with deadly tusks. Most people avoided them, but Muhumid actually sought them out. Using just a little wire, he would set snares in the woods. Sometimes one would get its foot stuck. Muhumid checked his traps every couple of days, hoping for a good dinner. The boar was tethered but not defenseless. Muhumid had to finish the job using his knife and a hatchet."

"You could tell just by looking at Muhumid that he was as tough as they come. His body was decorated with scars, and he wore them as proudly as a war hero wears his medals. He was a sturdy man, not particularly tall but solid," I said.

A young boy came out from behind the counter with four scanty plates of beans and bread and pushed them onto our table between the four of us. We all took a reluctant breath and picked up our dirty utensils.

I resumed our tales about Muhumid. "I didn't really know him all that well at first. He had been living at the house since I got there in the beginning of July. We worked together but we couldn't talk much. I just knew that he was a hard worker."

"How did you communicate with the language barrier?" wondered Mike. "How did you get anything done, let alone become such good friends?"

"Simple. Making friends is a lot more than being able to understand the words that come out of their mouths," Alex replied.

I started to explain: "We didn't have television at the house in Al Hoceima. There was no local hangout. We had a radio but the music they played was terrible, and any broadcast we wanted to listen to would only be understood by half of the people. After working hard all day, evenings were our time to relax. But there wasn't really anything to do and even talking with the other guys at the house was tough. I mean, on the job site my Arabic was good enough to communicate simple things, but as far as getting to know someone — sharing hopes, dreams, stories, and loves — that was much more difficult. Every evening we basically all sat around and looked at each other until we got tired enough to fall asleep.

"But it all changed the day that Muhumid found this drum called a *derbuka* that someone had left upstairs in one of the rooms. I would have never guessed it by looking at him, but Muhumid was quite the drummer. He had an amazing sense of rhythm. One night Alex and I were playing with Musha, the stray kitten we found in the road a couple weeks earlier, when Muhumid excitedly showed us his new find. At first we all just watched as he started thumping away, trying to find a beat. It sounded irregular and unnatural. Then, slowly, I started to hear it. It was different, unlike the conventional hip-hop beats, but it was there, his rhythm was coming. Always repeating, never quite catching up to itself.

"The other Moroccans started to perk up a bit and bob their heads. I looked at Alex and he could feel it too. We could collectively only understand about one third of the words that came out of Muhumid's mouth but now he was talking crystal clear, not with words but in a language that we could all understand. Alex flipped over the bucket he was sitting on. He waited, his head moving up and down with the beat. Muhumid was looking right at him, urging him to join the conversation. Alex let down his hand with a startling thud. It was out of place and not very pleasant sounding, but it didn't matter, the next one was closer. Thud ... thud ... thud ... thud. Before we knew it, he was right on beat. Two of the other Moroccans and I were all smiling now and scrambling for potential instruments. I was next to join in with a big pot and a spoon. The conversation grew louder, with the three of us talking, sharing things that we had thus far been unable to share. Next thing I know, the last two guys are slapping their hands on the round table in front of them.

"It's really true when people say that music is a direct line of communication from one person's soul to another's. When people play their hearts, they don't need to say a word. Certain music just resonates within us. Even a simple beat can express so much. We may not know the details of the musician's story, but we can feel what's going on inside of them."

"Yep," Mike said. "Wow, this food it terrible."

The rest of us crinkled our noses in consent.

"That night," I went on, "we were able to communicate. There was no language barrier, no divisions. We each had our beat, they were all different, but they fit together beautifully. For the first time we were a team.

"I didn't realize how significant our drum circle was at first. It went on for hours. We all went to sleep on our concrete beds a lot later than usual but the next morning everyone seemed to be rested and pleased with the work awaiting us. It's not that anyone had been uncivil or upset before that day, but there was a noticeable difference. I felt like now I was finally getting to know these guys. We had shared everything—we all slept on the same floor, we all ate from the same dish, we all bathed under the same spigot—but we weren't in tune, we weren't connected. Now everyone was playing the same song. I hadn't learned any more Arabic since the previous night, but now I felt like there was so much more substance being communicated with the little Arabic I did know.

"Right away Alex and I went out and bought some more drums, all different sizes. We were ready to jam again. The Moroccans were stoked. Our drum circle became as much a part of our nightly routine as sleeping. No matter who was there, whether they spoke Riffi, Arabic, Spanish, English, or French, they could become a part of the group if they wanted to. They could join the team for as long as they were staying in our home."

"That must have been really something, being able to live and work beside an entirely different culture and people," Kris said.

"It was amazing," agreed Alex.

✦

With lunch over, we loaded up, stopped by Josephate's shop, then hit the road. The Kenyan side of the border went without a hitch. So far, so good.

We got to the Ethiopian side, where Mike and I tried to buy our visas.

"Sorry, we don't issue visas; you need to go back to Nairobi."

Silence. I was ready to level this guy.

"We *went* to the embassy in Nairobi. They told us that we could buy them here."

"I'm sorry; they were misinformed. We can't let you pass without a visa."

Mike was shaking with fury. "Erik, I'm going through this border. I'm not going back to Nairobi."

We called our embassy in Ethiopia's capital, Addis Ababa, from a nearby pay phone and got hold of someone willing to help us. She called the head Ethiopian immigration office and explained our story.

We were sick with nervousness. The thought of having to travel back to Nairobi was unbearable; I don't think we could have survived that road again.

It was 3:40 p.m. In just twenty minutes the border would close and we would have to spend the night in no man's land, stuck between two nations.

That's when the phone rang inside the immigration office. It was the central office in Addis Ababa, authorizing them to issue us temporary visas.

Oh, thank God. We were in Ethiopia.

Oh, crap. We were in Ethiopia.

Is This the End?

Ethiopia

The scenery in Ethiopia was uniquely beautiful. Long, lone mountains were separated by wide-open land. There were no forests, just faintly tinted fields or semi-dry brush. We had gone up in elevation, so the air was crisp and cool. Nine-foot phallic-like ant pillars were scattered throughout the fields. It was as if the ants were having some sort of competition. "Mine's bigger!" "No mine is!"

Cattle, donkeys, and camels wandered unchecked through the region. The worst were the camels. These brainless animals would wander right out into the middle of the road, and when you got close they panicked. You could see in their faces how distressed they were. One might think that a startled animal would run from that which startled it—but no, not these camels. These camels were a bit special; they would run directly toward you as often as they would away.

We were flying down the road about 70 mph, thrilled to be on pavement again, when we rounded a corner and saw a huge herd of camels standing stupidly in the road before us. Alex was in the lead. He hit the brakes but wasn't going to be able to stop in time. The camels just watched him get closer until it looked like a collision was inevitable; then they broke out into a blind frenzy and ran aimlessly in all directions. Alex started dodging six-foot-tall camel butts, coming within inches of gaining firsthand knowledge of the dietary norms of Ethiopian camels. The sight was too hilarious not to laugh. But it was a close call.

We slept that night in a cheap guesthouse. Our rooms cost a whopping ten Ethiopian *birr* ($1.20) each. The following morning when we filled up on gas, the man responsible for pouring the buckets of petrol into our tanks tried to charge us for an obscene amount, far more than our bikes were even capable of carrying. After a less than friendly exchange, we were off. I already had a bad feeling about the day.

About forty miles later we came to a tight corner, swooping downhill to the right. Just off the left side of the road was a rocky but level shoulder, perhaps thirty feet wide, and then an abrupt dropoff into a valley full of boulders and scrawny trees. We were moving faster than we probably should have been: about 80 mph, Kris in the lead with Mike on the back of his bike.

The curve was tight but Kris managed. Alex saw it. It was clear he didn't think he would make it. I was following close behind him. He couldn't quite cut it. He turned, but not enough. He got closer and closer to the edge of the pavement.

"Hang on, Alex. Hang on!"

His tires hit the grass and jumped over the first rock. He went down hard, his bike sliding as he tumbled.

I needed to get to him.

I didn't think. In just a split second my window to make that turn had come and gone. I never even hit the brakes. I don't know what happened. Did I simply follow like a lemming, or did I think I couldn't make it, or was I just trying to get to my little brother as fast as I could?

Alex was almost done sliding; he was not going to fly off the edge. I just needed to crash quickly. I laid the bike down on its right side, my right leg momentarily pinned between the rocks and four hundred pounds of hot steel before I kicked myself free. I slid. I was on my back, feeling the rocks bounce under me. My helmet rattled like it was not even attached to my neck.

I have to get to Alex. Stop sliding. Get up.

I was still moving when I popped onto my feet. I hopped over to Alex's wreck. He was still lying on the ground, not moving yet.

The pain hit all in one big throb. I felt my skin try to jump off my bones. My right leg felt like it had been run through a grinder. With every heartbeat I felt it fresh. This was what Alex was feeling. He was hurting.

"Get up!" I said.

He just looked at me with wide, frightened eyes.

"Talk to me. Are you okay?"

"Erik, pray with me."

I did my best to squeeze out a couple words, begging God for Alex's safety.

"Erik, I think my leg is broken."

I just stood there immobilized until my body could figure out how badly I was hurt.

"You're alive; we'll figure the rest out. Don't you worry about a thing."

Kris and Mike had turned around, parked, and were running to us. Kris knelt and held Alex's leg.

"Erik, it might be broken," Kris said.

Mike and Kris both uttered a quick prayer.

Alex tried to stand. He winced but his leg could support his weight. He took a step, then another. He could walk. Maybe it was just a deep bruise?

"Just let me walk it off."

He just crashed a motorcycle going eighty. He wouldn't be able to walk it off.

Kris and Mike looked around and saw my bike in pieces fifty yards away. They realized that I had crashed too.

"You all right, Erik?" Mike asked.

"Just bumps and bruises, I think. You want to check out my bike?"

The whole right side was destroyed. My handlebars were bent backward and broken in half, both turn signals were gone, the mirror was smashed, the foot peg and back brake were completely ripped off. My bike looked a lot worse off than me.

Alex's bike was still rideable. He was walking with a bad limp, but thank God his leg was not broken.

Kris dug for the first-aid kit and found a bottle of iodine. The coffee-colored liquid lit our open wounds on fire as it mixed with fresh blood. Alex winced.

"You doin' okay?"

"I'm fine."

We sat on the side of the road helpless, stranded, waiting. A half hour passed before another vehicle, an empty truck, drove by. Kris ran into the road and waved the driver over. He agreed to take us to a village 160 km away for a reasonable fee. We all heaved my destroyed bike into the back of the truck.

I rode shotgun with the driver, working out all my bumps and bruises as best I could. Alex was in back stretching out to keep his leg as comfortable as possible. Kris and Mike shadowed us with the two good bikes.

An hour and a half into the drive, I was itching to get back on a bike. I went back to look at mine and saw that since loading it into the truck the gas tank had gotten all dented up. *What else, man?*

"Erik, when we get home and you go back out to the Air Force Academy, I'll fix up your bike like new," Alex promised. "Don't worry."

I wasn't mad about the gas tank. I didn't care about the gas tank. I was just tired, hurt, and, above all, worried. Once again Alex survived, totally unscathed, something that would have killed most people. I just wanted the trip to be done with. We had taken our journey; we had seen amazing sights and helped plenty of people. We had enough stories to keep our grandkids busy for hours. I just wanted to get home safely. We were starting to push our luck and I dreaded that it was going to run out.

How did I end up with a brother as gracious as Alex? I looked him in the eyes. "I don't care about the stupid gas tank. I just thank God you're okay."

We arrived at a little nothing town with nothing much in it, though the hotel was halfway decent. Fortunately, we were able to make friends with a welder and spent the rest of the day trying to repair the damages. Six hours of letting Alex loose with an oxyacetylene welder and my bike was running as good as new. Well, almost; I still didn't have a rear brake, but that was a minor detail. Alex and I were both pretty stiff, but operational. It was still a long road to Addis Ababa.

✦

Addis was a modern city with big buildings and good roads. We arrived after a full but uneventful day's ride and scavenged through town looking for a guesthouse cheap enough for us to afford. We didn't have much money left. Finally we stumbled upon a questionable looking place that rented rooms for forty-five Ethiopian birr a night (about five US dollars); during the day they charged by the hour. It was by far the cheapest place we'd come across. We took it. It didn't take long for us to realize that the "extra services" offered were what really funded this place. It was a brothel. Guys came in with their girls and enjoyed a nice cup of coffee and then "relaxed" in the rooms together. None of us were thrilled about the place, but it did provide a soft bed to sleep in and a dry roof over our heads. It would do.

With that task accomplished, we suddenly realized that we had reached the end. Addis Ababa was as far as we were going to take our bikes. To me the thought of packing these stallions into a container and sending them back to America was cause for both relief and melancholy. They had carried us so faithfully over eight thousand miles, through so many trials and tribulations, and now we were going to finish the journey without them. We all had a certain attachment to our bikes. They had become a part of us, just like we had become a part of one another.

Letting them go, however, may be just what we needed. We were all getting far too comfortable on those two-wheeled suicide machines. Despite every spill, we were pretty good riders by now, had been wearing all the proper protective gear, and knew every bolt on our bikes inside out; but the responsible part of me that I hadn't even known existed before now just wanted to get them out from under us.

Every day we scavenged through Addis trying to find a way to get our bikes home and get ourselves to Cairo. We investigated taking a ship around, but that route had been out of commission for years. We tried to find a shipping company that we could trust to send our bikes back to the States, but every day we discovered another false lead, another impossible obstacle.

Ahhh! I started to wonder if we would ever make it to Egypt. But I trusted. I mean, God had gotten us through impossible situations before. He had kept us alive through terrible places. If this trip was really his plan, and I never doubted that it was, then he would make something available. He would open some door. He always did.

For a week, as we continued our investigations, we usually treated ourselves to one real meal a day and then snacked on bread or lentil-filled pastries or potatoes for the other two. In a field beside one of the restaurants we even entered a foosball tournament with some Ethiopian laborers.

And, of course, we rode. One stretch of road that we particularly loved was right in the center of the city. It went straight down a very steep hill and then abruptly flattened out before dropping again. We hit it going about 60 mph every time and got launched through the air before returning to the pavement laughing. It was like being in a movie car chase.

We got to know many of the street children by name, mostly orphan boys wandering at all hours, begging for change at intersections or trying to sell tissues to motorists. These boys loved our motorcycles. They jumped and cheered every time they saw us approaching. Alex and I usually called one of them over whenever we stopped at a red light and let them climb onto the back of our bikes. We would go zipping through the streets and give them the ride of their lives. I can't think of too many things more rewarding than seeing those little guys' faces when we dropped them off afterward to a crowd of excited friends.

We had some good times in Addis, but we knew they were about to end. Kris was tired, still fighting the parasite he had picked up back in DRC. I was stressed about finding a solution to our transportation dilemma and kind of withdrew for a while. Mike was relaxed, knowing that we'd figure something out. Alex, as always, was easygoing and reasonable. When everyone else was down, we could count on him to cheer us up. He somehow managed to find a smile in even the darkest places.

At last we got good news—a shipping company would transport our bikes from Addis to New York. All we needed to do was drive them to a container and fill out the appropriate paperwork. What a relief. As soon as we agreed on the price, all of the tension, all of the frustration of the past week, melted away. I thanked the guys, especially Alex, for putting up with me during that time. And they made sure I knew they deserved it.

We still had a couple days before we needed to load the bikes into the container. We still had time to see Lalibela.

"Let's do it," Alex said.

One last motorcycle trip to the ancient stone city.

One of Lalibela's many secret places.

ONE LAST HURRAH

Northern Ethiopia

About five hundred kilometers of road separated us from the ancient rock-hewn churches of Lalibela. We had slept in and got a late start on the day's ride, wandering out of the brothel just in time for several Ethiopian businessmen to take their mistresses out for coffee. A line was already forming for our rooms. The morning was frosty but we dressed light, knowing that the hot afternoon sun was coming.

It wasn't long before we reached the northern outskirts of Addis. It felt good to be out of the city and back into unrestricted countryside. The fields were lush; huge long-horned cattle meandered alongside the road; here and there little shacks had smoke coming out the top; sometimes we'd see an occasional kid loitering around the otherwise undeveloped land. We were back on our bikes again, all taking turns in the passenger seat. We were free to think, free to breathe.

The beautifully paved roads wound their way north throughout the afternoon and into the early evening before we started climbing in elevation. Up into the mountains we went. It felt more like what I imagined Scotland to be than Ethiopia: grassy hills, big gray boulders. As we neared a ridge, we could see an expansive canyon to the west. To the east the land dropped dramatically into a purple twilight abyss. The air was freezing, but that was to be expected at ten thousand feet.

The people in Ethiopia were generally much more disagreeable than in most of the countries we had traveled through. Usually people would wave as we passed by. In Ethiopia, particularly northern Ethiopia, they ran up to the road and threw rocks or tried to kick at us, even when we drove as fast as 90 mph. Needless to say, we almost instantly disliked Ethiopia; Mike and Alex felt so strongly they kept a stash of projectiles in their pockets for people who displayed such negative hospitality.

Traffic was infrequent on these roads, especially traffic operated by white people. Come to think of it, I couldn't remember seeing another white person other than embassy personnel since Nairobi.

But as we crested the peak of this ridge, just before beginning our descent into the village where we would sleep that night, a Land Rover headed the opposite direction stopped beside us. Three smiling Italians stuck their heads out the window to greet us: Antonio, Miguel, and a lady whose name I didn't catch. Turns out they had driven up from South Africa along the east coast and were making their way back, hoping to travel through central Africa. We started exchanging stories and local knowledge we had picked up along the way as Miguel retrieved a bottle of coconut rum from his belongings and took a swig. He handed it to Mike.

"Here, it's warm!" Mike didn't hesitate to put the bottle to his lips.

For the next fifteen minutes we talked as the bottle got passed around. They had just toured Lalibela so they told us all about the sites as well as which roads were terrible and which ones were passable. They even gave us a much more detailed map that they had acquired at some point. As shadows grew, we sadly bid our new friends good-bye, gave them one more embrace, and mounted our bikes. Just as quickly as the happenstance party of Americans and Italians had started, it was over.

We had been traveling along the dry, windblown west side of the ridge. Now the road went straight into the mountain through a narrow, pitch-black tunnel. A sign above the tunnel said that it was built with the support of the European Union. As soon as we entered, the pavement ended and we were on a bumpy dirt road full of potholes. Partway through we saw two big round headlights coming toward us, and we squeezed against the right wall. A truck went flying by, filling the tube with a blinding cloud of dust. We idled forward, deeper into the black. Eventually we emerged on the other side of the ridge and into a wild new environment. The valley that we could barely see in the fading sunlight was moist, tree-filled, and accented by razor-sharp mountains. And at the bottom of the valley was our destination: a warm and welcoming little oasis.

We reached the guesthouse, exhausted. A cup of hot tea and a bowl of cold noodles put us right to sleep.

+

I was wide awake at 1 a.m. and then drifted in and out of sleep until my watch alarm broke the silence four hours later. It was still black outside—not a trace of light on the horizon. I got up before everyone else. I read, I wrote. I could hear the others starting to stir. As we got dressed and readied the bikes in the twilight that preceded the sunrise, an eerie purple-blue light faded into orange until finally the big red ball poked its face from behind the mountain in the distance.

The roads were not good—paved but in ill repair. Huge pointy mountains surrounded the expansive green meadows dotted with inviting-looking huts and cattle. Such a place made me wonder who among us is poor. I know a lot of people who would gladly trade their cubicle office and cookie-cutter home for such rugged, undisturbed beauty.

Up into the mountains we went along tarmac precipitously etched into the face of the cliffs, down into idyllic valleys separated by green deciduous forests; we rode and rode and rode as fast as we could. Occasionally old Soviet tanks, a relic of a time come and gone, lay broken beside the road, most long since stripped of anything of value, but some still sporting turrets and barrels. They were just part of the landscape and got no special attention now. The locals propped themselves against them as they would a large rock.

We drove for eight hours, stopping only once for fuel and food. We had ridden hard, but we still had a long way to go. All we knew was that the broken pavement we had been traversing had ended altogether. About 2 p.m. Kris's clutch cable snapped and we monkeyed with it an hour, rigging it up so that at least it worked—enjoying the break, but anxious to resume lest we get stuck that night in the middle of nowhere.

The terrain had become desertlike again. Camels were everywhere, hauling wood into the sparse villages. Several dried riverbeds cut up the roadways. Little boys wearing red clothes danced and played in these oversized sandboxes.

A couple more miles on switchbacks led us up another mountain ridge. Mike was on the back of Kris's bike. You could tell the bumpy road was killing him. Whenever we stopped, Alex and I offered to trade off with him, but he insisted on keeping his position.

"Quit being a tough guy, Mike. We'll rotate out with you, man."

"I'm not being a tough guy. I would rather suffer up here on the back of a bike that's going to stay on two wheels than trade off with you and crash a stupid dirt bike." Mike drove a souped-up crotch-rocket back in the States and hated driving a dirt bike on shifty terrain.

We rode up the pass, overtaking men with handmade tools and sticks, I suppose walking home from the day's work. Big families of baboons sat lazily on the side of the road and watched us go by. Ugly vicious things that growled and showed their teeth, they looked more like Big Foot than monkeys: flat faces, big boobs, long hair. Atop the pass the topography changed yet again to icy, barren rock fields. The air at this elevation — eleven thousand five hundred feet — was stark and dry. The road was loose gravel. We were making good time, but it felt like riding on water. A bit disconcerting at 65 mph.

By now, Mike was lifelessly slouched over on the back of Kris's bike, his arms bouncing totally limp at his side, his head bobbing apathetically up and down. He looked like a rag doll.

I pulled up next to him. "Hey, Mikey! You dead, man?"

His otherwise nonresponsive body lifted one arm and gave me a thumb's up before dropping back to its previous position.

We traveled down that road a total of 110 km, never sure that we were actually going in the right direction. Finally, just an hour before sunset, a turnoff — a road that went north and a sign indicating that our destination was 64 km away. We would finish in the dark, but at least we would finish. We flew down into the valley. I still didn't have a rear brake, and descending six thousand vertical feet on loose gravel roads around hairpin turns was a bit unnerving.

We arrived in Lalibela — after almost fourteen hours straight on our bikes — worn out, hungry, and dirty. We found a cheap guesthouse but decided to treat ourselves to a decent dinner at a nicer place. A couple of English speakers who no doubt flew into the new small airport just 15 km away were neat, comfortable, well fed, and going to sleep in a lovely bed that night. In one or two days they would fly away back to wherever they came from and tell people that they experienced Lalibela. They wouldn't have to travel an arduous road or worry about getting to Addis Ababa in time, in one piece. They weren't concerned about crashes. I didn't envy them.

✦

Lalibela is famous for a series of eleven churches carved from a single slab of granite in the late twelfth century. The legend goes that in the second half of the twelfth century God appeared to King Lalibela in a dream and told him to build a new Jerusalem in the middle of this remote region of northern Ethiopia. Archaeologists today say it would have taken a workforce of some forty thousand men to complete the project in the twenty-three years that historians tell us it was constructed. Some Ethiopians say that a thousand Egyptians came down to help. Most believe that angels came down from heaven and worked at night while the workers slept. Whatever the case, the builders chiseled these churches — some fifty and sixty feet high — out of solid rock. The corners are perfect, the edges straight, the arches and doors and windows elaborate. Archaeologists are still baffled.

This is Ethiopia's holy land, the religious capital of the country. Though Christianity arrived here in the fourth century, when Islam swept through this part of Africa in the seventh century, Ethiopia, virtually isolated from the rest of the Christian world, clung tenaciously to the faith. Christianity in Ethiopia looks a lot different than in the States. Monks have large metal crosses that they carry atop ancient-looking staffs; they kiss the church steps and chant prayers over and over; they crawl into the ancient tombs that have been carved into the stone walls that surround the churches and pore over their prayer books. In one of the tombs we found a pile of bones, the tendons dried but still clinging to the bones, with sun-dried human skulls atop the pile.

The buildings themselves demanded reverence. Alex looked in awe at the archways. Kris and Mike wandered through the endless doors and passageways. I could hardly take it all in. Inside one of the churches a monk stood guard in front of a tall archway with red linen hanging down to the floor. Through this archway was one of the two believed resting places of the ark of the covenant.

An intricate system of ancient tunnels connected all of the churches. Some were open, some had caved in, and some were simply covered by rusty iron gates. Kris and I slipped into one of the partially unobstructed tunnels. At some point over the centuries the ceiling had caved in but the tunnel wasn't completely blocked. We snuck deeper and deeper down into cold, black, stagnant air. Kris motioned for me to stop. He heard something up ahead making noises from inside the darkness.

"What is that? Is someone up there?" we whispered back and forth, still for the moment as we strained our eyes to identify the source of the noise.

Suddenly a cloud of bats engulfed us, flapping around our heads, squeaking at us to leave. We both dropped to our knees and buried our heads under our arms. Then, all at once, the bats shot deeper down into the tunnel. The tunnel was caved in up ahead and we decided it was time to emerge. Alex and Mike had been looking for us.

We spent the whole morning climbing through, around, over, and under this ancient labyrinth. By midafternoon, after having befriended a couple local boys and giving them rides around town, we pointed our bikes back toward Addis.

Two days later we were on a plane to Cairo.

At the pyramids (left to right: Alex, me, and Mike).

LIFE INTERRUPTED

Cairo, Egypt

Of all the travel warnings that we had ignored, Egypt's was the least threatening. It had been nine years since the last terrorist attack there. We flew into Cairo just like thousands of tourists do every day, checking into a cheap hotel full of other travelers. We took taxis to the great pyramids of Giza. We strolled through the souvenir shops looking for little trinkets we could spend a couple of dollars on.

I woke up early on our second day there. I always woke up first. As usual, Alex and I were roommates. He was sleeping in the bed beside me; Mike and Kris were just across the hall. It was too early to wake them. I read for a while in my warm bed, letting them sleep a little longer. We had another full day ahead of us.

Breakfast was cheap and not too good. I bought some local bean-based food from a street vendor and then brought it up to the restaurant. Alex had asked me to pick him up a juice while I was out, but it would have cost about a dollar, almost as much as our whole breakfast, and we didn't have that kind of money. I walked right by the juice vendor.

We filled our stomachs with the bean paste and flat bread. We were basically alone in the restaurant except for one other man in the corner watching the Arab equivalent of MTV on the only TV in the room. The music was terrible; the video was ridiculous. I wanted to go home. The hotel's restaurant was on the top floor and lined with windows. I think the idea was to offer the guests a view of Cairo, but the truth was that there wasn't much to see. Around us in every direction were narrow streets separated by gray, unfinished buildings with exhaust rising up from between them. It was not a pleasant sight by any stretch of the imagination. Right across the street directly in front of our hotel was the train station.

I didn't want to spend any more time in this dirty tourist trap than we had to, but we might as well make the best of our time and see all of the sites before leaving the city forever behind. Today we would tour all the wonders that Cairo boasted; tomorrow we would head south to the Valley of the Kings.

Our first stop was the impressive Cairo Museum where six-thousand-year-old men have found a new resting place behind double-paned glass. They were once kings, but there was nothing sacred about them now, their wilted naked bodies up on display. They had become yet another ploy to attract the masses and filch a few more dollars from the tourists. Had the ancient Egyptians been able to anticipate such an end, I'm sure they would have taken to burning their dead, not immortalizing them.

"Hey, look at this; another dead guy," Kris muttered as he pointed to yet another mummified corpse.

"Yippee."

We had come so far and seen so much. We tried to get excited about the museums and the history, but we didn't have much left in us. The last four months of sights, struggles, and adventures had used all the excitement we had.

It was time for our last stop in Cairo. "Where to now?" Alex prompted.

"How about the Khan al-Khalili marketplace?" I suggested. I had lived in the medina in Fez, Morocco, for a couple of months almost two years earlier. Fez was said to be the oldest functional medieval city in the world except for the Khalili marketplace in Cairo. I had to at least see it.

We hiked through the Cairo streets to a train station. For just a couple Egyptian pounds (around fifty cents) each, we crowded onto a train headed in the general direction of the marketplace. It was miserably hot in the train; our sweat mixed with the Egyptians' sweat everywhere our skin pressed against theirs. My back was soaked beneath my backpack.

When we finally exited the train we were still a couple miles from our destination, so we decided to eat a cheap meal before taking a taxi the rest of the way. The food wasn't much and left us all still hungry, but we were used to that. We waved down a taxi and negotiated a fare, but once at the marketplace the driver insisted we pay him more than we had agreed to. I was so sick of people trying to hustle us for a couple dollars, but I reminded myself that this was our last day in Cairo; in just two weeks we would be home celebrating this victory on Alex's birthday. No one even reacted to the driver's demands. Kris simply refused on behalf of all of us. The driver yelled something in Arabic as he drove away. We never turned our heads.

The sun was just starting to get low and the entire ground level of the medina was covered in shadows. Hundreds of busy people bustled from one shop to the next through the narrow, stone streets lined with three-story buildings on either side. About half of the crowd was Egyptian; the other half were complacent tourists like us. For the first time that day, a welcome cool breeze hit our still-sweaty backs, pushing us further into the marketplace. We wandered aimlessly through the labyrinth from shop to shop, searching for the perfect souvenir for the better part of an hour. It was twilight now. The sun must have been hovering just above the horizon. We couldn't see it from inside the maze.

"Let's get some dinner. I'm starving," Alex said. Tired from a day of sensory overload, we were ready for a decent meal and a restful night's sleep.

"Good call. We'll stop at the next place we see," I responded.

"How about that place?" Mike pointed to a little café that looked like it probably served food.

"Nah," Kris said as we all walked by.

We turned right onto a street. We turned right, not left, for I don't know what reason. Then we turned left onto another street. We turned left, not right, and I'm not sure why. We went straight. I don't know why we went straight.

This street didn't look any different than any other streets. It was narrow, full of people going about their business, carrying supplies from one shop to another, bringing groceries home for dinner. A small group of French-speaking tourists strolled on the other side, peering into one of the shops.

I looked back at Alex, who was glancing down. He noticed that I had turned around and looked up and forced a smile. This was not the highlight of our trip, but we were still glad to be here together.

Kris was the only one to notice that a young Egyptian man wearing black socks, clutching a bucket to his chest, had casually approached us coming from the opposite direction. He was passing by us on the left. As soon as he passed Kris, Kris heard a clicking sound, like someone trying to light a gas grill. He followed the boy with his eyes, trying to identify the noise.

Click . . .

Click . . .

Click . . .

BOOM!

Welcome to hell.

The explosion went off right in the middle of the four of us. Kris was looking at the back of the devil carrying the bomb, this young man's soulless body between him and the explosion. Fire engulfed my friend, burning off most of his clothes and charring his eyes and face. Mike was in the rear, the furthest from the blast. Between them were Alex and I. The brunt of the explosion hit us.

I had looked over my right shoulder to Alex not a second earlier, leaving my back, rather than face, exposed to the bomb, my spine and organs protected by the backpack I was wearing. Thousands of nails shot into the backpack and into my legs, arms, and skull. The blast blew me into a nearby alleyway where I lay unable to move. Alex was facing the bomb and took its full force, sending his one-hundred-and-fifty-pound body flying backward through the street.

We lay there silent. The buildings' normally gray walls were now painted red and black. All the windows lining the scene were blown out. Shards of glass were still raining from above. A light mist of blood filled the air, covering the street, the walls, us.

I took my first breath amidst the choking smoke, barely able to see a dozen other miserably deformed bodies scattering the ground. Some were moving; others were still. Screams erupted, breaking the silence. We were trapped in the smoke, in a sphere of destruction separated by an impenetrable wall of onlookers. The bodies in the sphere of destruction rolled and moaned. I was one of them.

Finally the ambulance starts to move. Turns and stops ... turns and stops ... turns and stops. I struggle to stay awake. If I go to sleep now I won't wake up. But I'm so tired.

Please let me stay awake. I have to fight.

"Hang in there, Erik," Kris says. "I'm here with you."

I hear Kris. But I don't have the strength to look.

Finally at the hospital, we are all put into a temporary holding area, no bigger than a college dorm room. I look around. Some of the people are more dead than me, some are less.

I am dying.

We all wait. Kris is on a stretcher in the same room. He is yelling at me to hang on.

"Erik, how you feelin', buddy?" It's Mike's voice. He's alive.

"Kris!"

"Yeah, Erik?"

"Mike's alive; he's here."

"I know, Erik; he's next to me. He's okay."

I don't care to force out any more words. Mike is alive. *Now where is my brother?*

Hands grab me and move me onto a cold, rolling steel table with a ripped-up rubber pad. As they cart me down a hallway, I hear screaming from one of the rooms.

It's my brother! It's Alex! Everything in him is screaming. "Ohhh God, ohhh God, ohhh God! Help me!" It is my dear Alex. They must be operating on him.

I pray the only prayer I have, for the only person I care about, for the only thing I need.

God, hear me now if you have ever heard me. In this time I have but one thing to ask you: Be with my brother and get him through this. God, let him be okay. Get him through this.

I shout, "Alex!"

Silence.

"Alex! I'm right here. I'm here, Alex! You're going to be okay!"

Silence.

"You hang on, Alex!"

Silence.

I am in another room now.

"Don't you die, Alex. You can't."

They begin to pull nails out of my body and cut off what little remains of my clothes. They soak me with cold water. I begin to shake uncontrollably. My breathing gets so shallow I can't get any air. My heart starts to flutter like a hummingbird in my chest.

"I'm … going … into shock …"

No one hears me. No one comes to help.

"Treat … for … shock."

Surely someone will see what is happening to me. Forget the nails. My system is shutting down. *Where are they?*

Nothing.

I am on my back looking up into the light. It gets brighter and then dims. Brighter still and then dim. It is blinding white and now black.

This is it. I'm dying.

People always tell stories about a white light to guide us or some divine encounter to comfort us as we leave this life. I can't see a thing.

I feel my body shutting down, my consciousness slipping away. No dead loved ones come to comfort me. No angels. In my final moment I am alone.

If I pass out now, I will never wake up again. Alex will have to live his life alone. All our plans, all our dreams—I won't be there for him. They begin to roll me to another room. No one speaks English.

Not yet, I'm not done yet.

I reach out with my right arm—the one limb I can still move—summoning all the strength I have left to grab a sheet off an operating table. I cover myself and try to breathe. They leave me alone. Have they given up on me? Am I already dead?

I'm not dying on Alex. I won't be another number for those soulless demons to boast of.

Fight!

Breathe. Just breathe.

Breathe.

Slowly, breath by breath, my lungs fill with air. *Just keep breathing.* Eventually the shaking stops.

Keep breathing. The pain is back. God, it hurts to fight.

Just keep breathing; don't give up.

They come and jam a hose into my penis. It robs me of my breath.

They stick a knife into my abdomen just below my belly button. I feel the knife go in and cut through my skin. They cut open my belly. I feel fingers reach inside of me. This is why Alex was screaming. They did this to him. God, it hurts so much.

I hear the word "morphine" uttered on the other side of the room, the only comprehensible sound in a slur of Arabic.

I shout that word over and over: "Morphine, morphine, morphine, morphine."

A man comes with a big needle and sticks it into my neck. The pain doesn't go away but suddenly I am indifferent to it, blissfully indifferent. Everything slows down. I shut my eyes.

✦

A woman comes into focus from inside the blurry room. She is speaking to me in English. A large black man is next to her. They are both American. I don't know them, but they care about me.

"Erik, you're okay. We're from the embassy. We're going to stay with you."

I could barely whisper. "Where is my brother?"

They try to ask me a question. I can't understand them.

"Where is my brother?"

"He is here," the woman calmly tells me.

"Is he okay? Take me to him."

"He's not doing very well, Erik. The doctors are with him."

"Is he gonna make it?"

Silence.

God, not silence.

"IS HE GOING TO LIVE?"

She hesitates. "Erik, it doesn't look good."

"Where is he? Take me to him. Take me to him! TAKE ME TO HIM!" The woman starts to tear up.

The black man is very angry. He is yelling at the hospital staff in Arabic.

"Erik," the woman says, "you are in bad shape; we need to move you to another hospital or you are going to die."

My eyes close.

✦

I remember back to nearly two years earlier when I had come home for a couple of weeks before heading off to Morocco. I could see clearly that Alex was very upset about something. He finally explained to me that a punk who called himself his friend was spreading lies about Alex cheating on his girlfriend. Apparently this guy was after Alex's girlfriend and was trying to break them up. Alex's girlfriend would call him crying, asking if any of the talk was true. My brother had been anguishing over the situation, trying to decide how to handle this kid.

As the big brother just out of military school, I was furious that someone was causing my brother such distress and offered what seemed to me like the obvious solution.

"Let's get in the car and go beat this kid down right now."

But Alex, somewhat quietly and unmoved by his own frustrations, said only, "You know what, Erik? We could drive over there and beat this kid, but that would just give him a cause to keep talking and it would validate some of the things he's saying about me."

"Well, what are you going to do? You can't let this continue."

He paused for a moment, looked at me, and said, "I'm not going to do anything about it. I'm not going to say anything to anyone. Anyone who knows me will know that he is lying between his teeth when he talks about me, and anyone who believes him doesn't know who I am anyway. My character is strong enough to speak for itself. And anyone I care about knowing is smart enough to see what is going on here."

I was speechless. I knew then that my brother was not just an ordinary kid. He was right too. After a while people got sick of hearing this punk talk about Alex. Alex didn't need to defend his name because others were there to do it for him. Eventually whenever this other guy opened his mouth, a host of people were ready to call out his lies for what they were and expose him for who he was.

That was but one example of my teenaged brother's remarkable character. It was his unmistakable character, not just his athleticism, that got him voted captain on the track and field team at one of the largest high schools in Michigan. It was his character that won him fifth place at the state finals while working five nights a week and going to school full time. It was his character that earned him the Pat Paterson Award for leadership, given to one varsity athlete a year at our high school. It was his character that gave him the strength to leave the loving comfort of home and venture out on his own. It was his character that sustained him as he pondered life's most profound mysteries of purpose and faith over the months of traveling the dark roads of Africa. He would make it, he was too strong to die.

+

I wake up. I have lost all concept of time. A woman doctor and a man are standing over me. They are both Egyptian.

"Where is my brother? Take me to him!"

"Your brother is in this room with you. Look over there; you can see him," the man says soothingly.

I strain my body. I summon all my strength and lift my head. Across the room lies a man, his head wrapped in white bandages, his body covered with a sheet. He is motionless, but I can tell it is my Alex.

"Take me to him! Take me to him!"

"You're going to another hospital now. The best hospital in Egypt," the doctor says.

"I'm not going anywhere without my brother. Let me talk to him!"

"We're going right by him; you can talk to him on the way." I relax a bit. They start rolling me toward the door. Soon I will stop next to my brother. I will be able to touch him and talk to him. Wait, I am going through the doorway! I passed right by my brother and didn't even look at him.

"WHERE IS HE? I DIDN'T TALK TO HIM! I WON'T LEAVE. TAKE ME BACK!"

"Your brother is right behind you. He is coming with you on the next ambulance. You will be able to talk to him at the other hospital, but we need to get there as soon as possible."

You lying son of a ...

I pass out.

+

I wake up in the ICU of another hospital. I don't remember much. It is light outside, but my room is dark. I can see people walking by the door. They stop, talk to each other, and keep walking.

"HEY! HEY! Come in here and talk to me!"

The door opens.

"Where is my brother?"

"He is still at the other hospital."

"Get me a wheelchair."

"You can't be moved."

"GET ME A WHEELCHAIR!"

I try to pull myself out of the bed onto the floor. I'm not strong enough. The pain is so great.

The man runs from my room. A doctor comes in. "What do you need, Erik?"

"Here is what I NEED. I do not need this bed or these tubes. I am fine. What I need is to know where my brother is. I need to be with him."

"They told me that he was too critical to be moved."

"Fine, then I need to go to the other hospital. I need a wheelchair."

I try again to move, and the pain shoots through my body. A prisoner. I can do nothing. The doctor leaves.

I lay there.

I wait.

I scream, but no one comes. I rip out wires and tubes. The alarms scream with me. They listen to the alarms but not me. Nurses come in to fix what I've done, but they won't talk to me.

Hours pass.

People from the embassy come to me and give me the phone. My parents are on the line. They are crying.

"Erik, how are you? Are you okay?"

"Don't worry about me. I'm fine. Where is Alex? Have you heard anything? They took me away from him. They lied to me." The phone cuts out.

"Hey! Hey! Your phone dropped the call! Get in here!" The embassy workers come in and call my home again. They all leave me alone in the room with the phone. As soon as my parents answer, the phone cuts out again.

"Move me to the window."

We call again. They leave me alone. My mom is crying.

"Erik, Alex didn't make it. He's dead."

"What? He can't be dead." *I'm supposed to be dead. How can he be dead?*

Tears explode from my eyes. My soul dies.

"I'm so sorry, Mom. I'm so sorry, Dad. I did the best I could. We weren't anywhere we shouldn't have been. I was watching. I never even saw it coming. He came from nowhere. I did everything I could. Alex was the first person on the ambulance. I sent Kris to be with him until the ambulance came. I thought he was going to be okay. I'm so sorry; I'm so, so sorry."

"It's not your fault, Erik; you just stay strong. Your mom and I will be there tomorrow night, but it's going to be very late. We'll see you soon."

"You just hang in there," Mom says.

"We have to go now. Our flight leaves soon."

"I'm so sorry, Mom. I'm so sorry, Dad."

"Just hang in there. We love you."

The lady from the embassy comes and gets her phone.

"Are you okay, Erik? Is there anything I can do?"

"Please shut the door and don't let anyone disturb me."

There is no hope for me anymore.

All that I care about is already lost.

My reason for fighting.

My life.

All in vain.

GIVE ME DEATH

Various Hospitals

Kris could see that Alex was hurt that day in Cairo, but on the outside he looked better than I did. The real damage was hidden inside. His spleen was ruptured and bleeding fast. His left lung was completely collapsed and filling with blood from the intense concussion. Most of his organs were severely contused, like someone threw all of his insides off a cliff and then jammed them back into his body. It was amazing he was still breathing at all. His carotid arteries were bleeding down the inside of his neck and blood was mixing with urine in his bladder.

I couldn't help imagining it: he lay there, unable to move, fighting for each breath. He knew that he was dying in a faraway land, in an unfamiliar place surrounded by people who couldn't even offer him a kind word or prayer.

Knowledge of his death marks my turning point. I start slipping further and further into death's grasp myself. He hasn't given up on me yet. He is waiting for the right time to claim me.

The doctors talk quietly. Everyone's face tries to hide it. The doctors are discussing amputating my left arm. Most of my triceps is gone anyway. It won't be much good.

The doctors don't think that I will ever walk again.

Lying on the pillow hurts and I discover I have a couple of nails sticking out of the back of my head. I tell the doctors, but they are convinced they're just burns. I apathetically pull them out of my skull with my one good arm.

Hundreds of nails are riddled throughout my body, each carrying millions of infectious bacteria. For two days the surgeons treat my visible wounds. I am still in critical care, but I have temporarily stabilized. The dressings on my wounds soak through with blood and begin to smell sickly sweet, like my broken body has begun to rot. While the doctors ignorantly watch my stable vitals, the bacteria multiplies and creeps ever so subtly into my blood stream. From there the disease has access to every cell in my body.

In just one day my system turns septic and I develop a terrible fever. Death is preparing his final assault. My dad and my mom, a nurse by profession, make it to Egypt just before things take a sharp turn for the worse.

For two days they watch my fever climb. They pump me full of every suitable medicine they have, but nothing works.

I am breathing, but my body's ability to absorb oxygen is dropping fast. My left lung isn't respirating and my right lung is quickly filling with fluid. My system is infected with all sorts of diseases—some treatable, some not. My temperature continues to skyrocket. I am just a couple degrees away from being brain dead. All of the organs that aren't directly involved with getting oxygen to my brain are shutting down.

I am going to die unless I receive better care. The only option is a military transport to Germany. It is a long shot but if I am going to survive the night they have to get me on that plane.

Death is getting ready to make his claim.

They want to put me into a coma to get my temperature down, which is risky in my current state, but they've tried everything else and my body can't fight anymore. An induced coma is my last chance, that and getting air evacked out of Cairo. They need to get that transport.

The doctors rush in to take me. My mom's eyes are full of tears. My dad is standing right beside her.

"I love you, Erik. You hang on," she urges.

"Don't worry about a thing. I'll be back in no time," I optimistically respond with a smile. I don't want the last memory of their son to be one of him hurting.

"You did a good job, Erik; now you get to rest," was the last thing I hear on my way out the door.

The doctors rush me down the halls and into the freezing operating room. They put a plastic mask over my face and inject the white liquid that makes all the pain stop. I can taste it entering my body.

Don't let me go.

The lights flash and then go black. Just darkness now.

✦

I am not afraid of death. Not because I am sure of what will happen after taking that fateful step from life—even the most outspoken of religious people couldn't claim that knowledge. I have my faith and its promises, but I also have a freshly sprouted inkling of doubt.

Neither is it because I am brave. People often confuse the fearless with the brave. There is a distinct difference. The brave force themselves to cope with fear for a cause. The fearless can *look* brave, but the fearless can never *be* brave.

I am not afraid of death simply because to die will mean an end to my fight. I am afraid, yes, but what frightens me most in this moment is the thought of waking up, of having to endure one more moment away from home, one more needle, one more breath that will send pain shooting through my body, one more dressing change, one more realization of having to live my life alone without the companionship of my dear brother. My injuries are permanent. I will probably never walk again. I may lose my arm. I will never be the same. I will stumble through the rest of this life a cripple, forever scarred both inside and out, far beyond any hope of healing. Oh, to die — what a blessing it would be! Don't make me have to quit to die. Spare me the torment that is to come.

But it is not that simple. My family has lost one already. At this moment my parents, grandparents, cousins, all my loved ones, and others who I have never even met are lying awake praying that I will survive. They can't see it like I see it. They would never know that my death is welcomed, not a punishment. They would have to cope with the death of another loved one. My poor mother — she would be all alone. No one would visit her on the holidays; no one would call her every Sunday night and tell her of the latest adventure. She would have nothing. If I died, she came with me.

My dad, could he bear the loss of both of us?

My baby brother, Jake, would grow up his whole life never knowing his older brothers. Erik and Alex would exist only in distant fairy tales that would be forgotten in time. I can't die. I have to fight.

As I drift through the impalpable grayness that separates life and death, I call out to God from the depth of my soul. I reach out for the slightest encouragement. I wait and I hope for an out-of-body experience, a divine encounter, a sign, any reason to believe that I am not fighting this battle alone. This is my darkest hour. All that I have is lost, all that I love is taken. If I have ever needed God, it is now.

I walk to the very edge of life and I peer into the darkness that lies beyond. I call out to its creator, to the God I had committed my life to.

My answer is this:

Empty silence.

In my moment of greatest need I am alone, forsaken, betrayed.

✦

A forced breath prompted by a soulless machine jerks me from the blissful void; back into that broken body, back into the struggle. The room is full of people. My family is here. I can see my mom and my dad, some others. I recognize some faces from church. They look tired. It must be late. The room is dark.

I remember the explosion. I remember the screams. I remember the smells. I remember what I saw. I remember the pain, the excruciating pain. In the movies when people are being tortured, they always pass out because of the pain. People always say that after you get injured you don't feel the pain because you're still in shock. I felt every nail that ripped through my body. I felt every chunk of flesh that had been blown off my body. I felt every nail sticking out of my head. I never passed out. Shock didn't numb what I felt. And now I was awake again, no better off than when I left this body of mine.

I try to speak, but the plastic tube stuck down my throat makes me gag. I am awake. I can breathe. I don't need this machine. I try to pull it out. My mom stops me with a touch.

"Erik, we got the plane. We're going to Germany. Hang on. Tomorrow you'll be in the best care in the world. Mike and Kris are going too. They'll be on the plane with you."

I was semi-sedated during the ambulance ride to the airport, pulling onto the tarmac, the flight to Germany. I have images in my head—just vague thoughts that don't go in any certain order.

I wake up in a German hospital. Three hours after I land I am in the operating room. They strip all my wounds and scrub the infections; they start to remove more nails. They pump my system full of antibiotics.

Within a day I stabilize.

The battle for my life has been won. Now all I can do is wait.

The doctor enters.

"Are you going to take my arm?"

"No, Erik, you're keeping it."

"How long until I can walk again?"

"It's not going to be easy, Erik. We don't know how much of this is permanent and how much will heal."

Now it is a matter of enduring the months it will take to recover. Now my greatest challenge isn't death—he has given up on me. Now it is the doubt, the questions that will be my company during these lonely hours to come. If only I had gone when I was still confident that God was in charge; before the endless nights of insomnia; before I had a chance to really question what I had accepted to be true; while still ignorantly convinced there was a light on the other side of this tunnel, that God was good, and that we all have a place in some perfect plan that he is orchestrating.

Every second hurts. I never have a chance to rest. At night the nurse comes into my room every fifteen minutes to draw blood to monitor the infections. Every four or five minutes some alarm sounds. During the day I try to move. Eventually I try to eat again. My six-foot, one-hundred-sixty-five-pound body has withered to a hundred and thirty-five pounds since the explosion. I am a skeleton.

Two painstaking weeks pass and I am stable enough to go back to America, back to the city I grew up in. Back to Grand Rapids.

It is here that I first hear the words "comfortable" and "pain management" in regard to my situation. They pump my veins full of the best synthetic heroin money can buy every four hours. It is my warm sunshine. It lets me feel nothing. I need it.

I start taking my first steps toward walking again. I have hoses and tubes hanging out of every hole. Four are attached to my shrapnel wounds, one is an IV, three hoses have been punched through my ribcage into my lungs (one got there using no anesthetic). My arms and legs are still filled with dozens of nails. My legs haven't done anything but bleed for a month. It's time to walk. It hurts to stand on them.

The physical therapists rush to help me. "Erik, hold on to the walker!"

"Get that thing away from me!"

"You can't stand without it!"

"I DON'T NEED A WALKER!"

One step. Two steps. Three steps. Don't tell me I can't.

+

My brother's body is flown back to Grand Rapids. They have the funeral, but I can't leave the hospital. Hundreds of people attend, but not me.

"NURSE! I need my drugs."

My warm sunshine.

More days. More nights.

I lie to the doctors about my pain so they will let me out of the hospital sooner. When it's a ten, I say two; when it's a five, I say I'm comfortable. *Let me go home.* I can stand by myself now and move from a bed to a chair and back. But without the help of IV narcotics, nothing moderates the pain. Every second of every day I live in pain, but at least I'm out of the hospital. No one will try to stop me from going on my walks. No one will tell me all the things I can't do. My mom knows me better than the hospital staff. My dad will walk with me.

At night I lie down on my back and stare at the ceiling. I watch TV. I read books. I do everything but sleep.

Nails continue to surface. They poke at my skin from the inside. I open the skin and pull the invasive little bastards out. They have no right to be in me.

The insomnia has begun. I am always tired. All day I am exhausted. As soon as I lie down I start to fall asleep and then wake up and stay awake. Every night I am alone.

The inkling of doubt continues to grow. I prayed to God so much over the last several weeks since the explosion. I prayed for my brother's life, I prayed for just a bit of relief from the pain, I prayed for any reassurance that I was not fighting this battle alone.

Give me a reason to want to hope.

Every one of my prayers has gone unanswered. Yet I am still breathing. It seems cruel. We were following his plan. We were doing what we believed we were meant to do. We never had any doubt that God was with us until that day in the market. I can't understand it. I survived against insurmountable odds. My body is healing. Doctors look at my charts in awe.

"Erik, it is an absolute miracle that you are breathing today."

I should have died from loss of blood after the bombing. By the time I got to the hospital I barely had enough left to keep my heart pumping. Twice I experienced irreversible shock. Irreversible shock is fatal; you're not supposed to survive it once, let alone two times. The diseases in my blood should have killed me. My whole body was shutting down when they wanted to transport me. My lungs had stopped absorbing oxygen. Just that one thing alone kills 75 percent of young, strong patients. Somehow right before I had to leave on the ambulance I stabilized just enough, and just long enough, to be moved. People are still trying to figure out how I managed to get that military transport from Cairo into the best military hospital in the world, the place normally reserved for our critically wounded soldiers.

I am as hardheaded as they come and I was determined to fight for my life as long and as hard as it took, but my survival was due to a lot more than my determination. It was a lot more than the doctors' touch. My consciousness was being guarded. My breath was being protected. Events lined up perfectly, so that I might live. I know beyond any doubt that the same force that I had followed to Africa, that led me through the marketplace that day, was keeping my heart pumping when death was imminent.

But we are so much more than the air we breathe. A person needs more than just a heartbeat. He needs purpose, he needs faith, he needs to know that he is not alone. I cannot figure out why God would protect the shell in which I reside but leave me completely alone when I need him the most.

For the months of recovery following the explosion I try to pray to God but my prayers are nothing more than an empty voice echoing inside my head.

Eventually I stop.

A reservoir outside Fez, Morocco.

A LIFE WORTH LIVING

Michigan and Hawaii

The sun rises every morning and sets every evening. Life doesn't stop; it doesn't wait for us. The world hurries about its business as if nothing has changed.

Everything has changed.

Months pass and I can walk again. I go in every few weeks for surgery. I still have fifty or so nails in my body. One by one the doctor takes them out. As soon as I recover from surgery, I go back in and do it again. I will never be like I was—strong and healthy—though few notice the difference. My scars are deep, but a nice shirt and a fake smile hide them well.

The school year has started. Kris is back out West attending university. Mike and I have nowhere to go, nothing to do. We just sit, wait, and heal. If only it were that easy. We are both taking classes in the city we grew up in. He lives just down the street from me. We are neighbors again, living with our lovely moms, just like when we were kids.

Mike talks about that day. When he regained consciousness there in the street, he was witnessing a wall of smoke and destruction, only fifty feet from the rest of us but separated by a daunting barrier. He saw the bloody holes in his arm, he felt the blood on his face, he looked at the destruction, at the bodies littering the street, and he knew beyond any doubt that he was the only one of us to survive. A crowd rushed around him. A couple locals grabbed him and hurried him away to the hospital. We were gone. Trying to find us was nonsensical. Mike's shocked mind was convinced that we were dead. He was on the outside, alone. We were trapped on the inside.

Everyone likes to think that if they were ever made to face the most calamitous of situations that they would behave a certain way. Tough guys always talk about what they would do if a robber dared to stick a gun in their face. I hear people critique frontline soldiers in Iraq from the comfort of their living room sofa while watching the evening news. Those people who have never been truly tested in the direst of circumstances have no idea what they would do if it were them alone, surrounded by death; when there is no crowd to applaud their valor or sneer at their cowardice. Those people have no right to judge the actions of the relative few who have been subjected to such a horror. And the few who have been tested and can vividly recall their reactions seldom speak of them.

News reporters love to tell our story. Around every corner is someone who recognizes us, who has heard about the Cairo bombing. They have come to know this Erik Mirandette, this Mike Kiel, and this Kris Ross who exist in newspaper articles and church bulletins and news flashes. These three men are wise, they have answers, their faith has sustained them. We are not those three men. We are lost, we are confused, we are angry, we are brokenhearted. We have lost our brother, and we are all alone.

Every morning the sun rises and brings with it another day in this dismal city. I watch my classmates rush through the week. Friday is coming. It is their goal, their hope. They will devour the trivial distractions that await them. They will gulp their noxious drinks, convinced that all is well. They cannot possibly imagine the horror that is now a part of me. I am so envious of them.

Another drink numbs my senses. Another conversation about that girl's scanty outfit fills a slot in my consciousness that otherwise would be left to ponder questions that have no answers.

Another sleepless night.

My phone rings. It's Friday night. Another party on campus. I'm driving and Mike is sitting in the passenger seat of my jeep.

"Do you want to go?" I say to him.

"Sure, but let's get a beer first."

We stop off at a nearby restaurant and find a secluded seat at the bar.

"Two of whatever your special is."

"Do you want talls or shorts?"

"Talls," we answer in unison.

The tension has been building all week. I've seen Mike hardly at all the past few days. I haven't been able to vent gradually, as is healthy. Usually I could go a week before I needed to get it out, but now the pressure is so high I'm about to burst.

Too much thinking is my problem. My mind has been clear and so the questions, the doubts, have come racing back to the forefront of my being. Soon I will bury them again. Mike is here to help me. I am here to help him. Soon.

"I bumped into some people from church yesterday," I say.

"Yeah?"

"They are still convinced that God will never forsake you. That in your time of need he'll be there for you."

"Maybe they're right."

I haven't slept in two weeks. I lie awake night after night—crying, furious, frustrated, defeated. Can't God offer me mercy even now? Forsaken is the only word I have. When I needed God the most he left me. Mike knows this. I don't need to waste time telling him again.

"Maybe."

"Maybe they're not." His words echo my thoughts.

"Oh, and get this. Someone I had never met caught me in the mall yesterday. Do you know what he said?"

"What's that?"

"'Wow, look at you. You look great. Isn't our God great? He is so merciful! You are a walking miracle!'"

My brother was killed in front of my eyes; my body was blown to parts. The pain of recovery has been excruciating. For four weeks I lay on my open, bloody back and butt. I couldn't move without pain. The grief of losing my brother has been unbearable. I fought for life, not because I longed to live but because I didn't want my loved ones to endure my death and I didn't want some terrorist to claim me as a victory. Death would have been bliss.

And yet they say that God was merciful for sparing my life?

If such is God's mercy, then give me wrath.

"Those are my favorites. What did you say?"

"What could I say? I said, 'Amen, brother; thanks for the prayers.'"

"That's about all you could say. He wouldn't have understood had you said anything else, anyway."

Our frosty brews come. We both dive in, soaking every little bubble up into our brains. Mine is half empty after the first swallow. Mike's is a bit lower.

"Have you ever thought about the word 'miracle'?" I ask.

"What do you mean?"

"Miracle. Have you ever thought about what it means? An event or series of events so astronomically improbable that it requires divine intervention to explain."

He just looks at me.

"But what is the word's opposite?" I continue. "The word always has a positive connotation because the divine is assumed to be good. But what if that is not the case?"

"What do you mean?"

"Is it any less of a miracle that after all of the dangers of Africa, a terrorist happened to blow himself up right next to us in a country that hadn't had a terrorist incident in over nine years. I say our getting bombed is just as much of a miracle as my surviving. How can people see the good and praise God for it and be completely oblivious to the terrible? Should that be credited to God as well? Should we curse him for the horrible as we praise him for the good?"

"Most people don't think about things like that, Erik. Most people give Satan credit for the evil. I don't know if that's right, but that's what most people do."

"You're right, and then they parrot something about this all working together for a greater good."

The devout tell me that this is part of God's greater plan. That it is hard to understand but it will all work together for the greater good. That already this event is having a profound impact on the Christian community. That lives are being changed and people are finding faith as a result of what happened to Alex. People need to get shaken to find God.

We knew God, we pledged our lives to God, and he demanded the highest price. Yet people are shaken, people are moved, and people are coming to him.

Alex could have been killed in a car wreck during his freshman year of college or in a motorcycle crash in Africa or gunned down in Congo. Nobody would have cared. But he wasn't. It was a suicide bomber in Egypt. How did we survive so much and die when it was least likely? It couldn't be chance; it couldn't be coincidence. So what does that mean?

Was it part of the bigger plan?

If so, to hell with the bigger plan.

Were we just in the wrong place at the wrong time?

Is it worth it?

Do I care? Maybe I would rather have a life with Alex and without God.

Would it have been any easier if it were a car accident that killed my brother? No one would have cared and I wouldn't have to question God. I would have accepted it as stuff that happens in a messed-up world. A simple cliché may have been enough of an answer.

Maybe what happened was directly from Satan and broke God's heart as much as mine. But he could have stopped it.

Ahh, the questions. I finish my beer with my second gulp. My mind is already starting to slow down.

"Hey, bartender, two more talls."

The bartender nods and starts to fill two new glasses. Mike finishes his beer.

I don't care. I want my brother. I would have given anything to take his place that night. Any of us would have. He was the first on the ambulance. It's not that God asked too much from me; he didn't let me do enough.

"Erik. Erik."

"Huh, what?"

"Come on back. There's nothing where you were letting yourself go. Stay here."

The next two drinks are standing in front of us.

"Maybe God is a surgeon, Mike. Maybe right now we're on the operating table. To stop before this operation is completed would be cruel. But could the greater good possibly justify such torments?"

I open the hatch and pour the icy drink into my stomach. It chills me.

"Maybe bad stuff just happens, Erik. Maybe sometimes no amount of figuring will make sense of it."

"Maybe you're right."

My mind begins to swim. Soon the questions will stop.

"You know what my greatest fear is, Mike?"

He knows the answer, but he asks me to continue anyway. He knows it's almost over. He braces himself against his fresh beer.

"My fear is not that God doesn't exist. I know God exists. My fear is that there is more to his nature than justice, peace, love, and joy. Is it unreasonable to describe God as cruel, unjust, partial, fickle, egocentric ... ?"

If not, then what is there to differentiate heaven and hell?

Nothing is certain, and no amount of thought will resolve my dilemmas. Thinking just leads me deeper down the tunnel, unleashing more doubts, calling more of what I know into question.

I finish my drink. I've made it—finally enough to stop my mind from racing.

Mike can see it in my face. "Welcome back. It took you a lot longer than usual."

"I know, it's taking more and more to slow me down. It's getting worse."

"This time will pass, Erik. Just hang in there."

"I've got to get out of here, Mike. I've got to get out of this city."

If what I had believed isn't true, if God is not the loving God I thought I knew, then my life and my brother's death are for nothing.

I'm torn; to quit would be so easy, such a welcome relief. I could crawl inside of this bottle and never come out. My cupboard is full of painkillers. They numb more than the physical. I can't believe that I haven't taken them all already. They are so tempting.

Yet to turn my back on life now would be to waste it all—all that I've lived for, all that Alex died for. To turn my back on it now is to deny that there is hope. I might as well have died in the street that day. Like it or not, my time on this planet is not over yet. And so I press on—where I'm not sure, but I can't stay here. Death and destruction are all that await me here.

"I need to get away and figure this stuff out. I can't do it here."

Mike looks at me, takes a deep breath. "So where are we going?"

"We?"

"Erik, there's no way I'm going to let you try to do this on your own. You need somebody watching out for you and you need to leave. So where are we going?"

"You don't need to do this, Mike."

"Whatever, man; you don't need to waste your breath."

"We're going to get lost. Someplace where no one will know our names, somewhere no one will recognize our faces."

"I hear Kauai is nice."

"Kauai it is."

"You ready to go to that party now?"

"Yeah."

✦

It's been over three years since I took that fateful step from the comfortable structure of university, with the promise of a commission, into the dark unknown by boarding a plane bound for Africa.

I still get updates every now and then from Manolo and his family. The last time that I was arrested in Morocco I was given an ultimatum: either abandon the refugees altogether or be forever exiled from Morocco. I listened to the counsel of those who I was there to help and I gave up my project on the mountain. A couple of months later I relocated to Al Hoceima. The refugees were gone. There was nothing more that I could do. However, their circumstances only worsened as their numbers grew.

Manolo was not so easily discouraged. Now, long after that first trip we took to Gurugu together, Manolo continues the work. While the border patrol scrupulously watched my every move in the months following the arrest, they completely missed the caravans of Spanish men and women, trunks full of supplies, who had suddenly developed a habit of "picnicking" on Gurugu once a week. Manolo spread the vision and it caught like wildfire throughout the Spanish communities. Since then the effort has grown into far more than we had ever anticipated. Led by Manolo and his family, entire church congregations in the local area have adopted the refugees on Gurugu.

In the past three years thousands of men, women, and children have been directly impacted by their love. The naked have been clothed, the hungry have been fed, the sick have been cared for, and the defeated have been uplifted. Lives have been saved.

Hundreds of people in Al Hoceima were hysterical when they heard about what happened to us in Cairo. Entire villages mourned Alex's death, reduced to tears upon hearing the news. All denounced the hate that committed such an evil.

Today people still tell stories about two courageous brothers, whose love was absolutely infectious, who came from a world away to help them when they needed it most.

The last four months that I had with my brother, we traveled through the most amazing and adventurous places and circumstances that exist. We lived life to the absolute fullest.

The decision that Alex and I made to follow our hearts and the time that followed was not in vain. I know that we were playing our part in the beautiful symphony that is being orchestrated all around us everyday.

So, was it worth it?

I still have a lot of unanswered questions. A lot of things will never make sense to me. I may never have quite the faith that I used to have. I will live the rest of my life deeply scarred both inside and out.

If I had known three years ago that embracing my purpose and helping my brother to live out his would have cost me his companionship, I would have never set foot on that plane. I would have never even thought about it. I would have without a second thought or hesitation thrown my destiny right out the window and preserved the comfortable life that I was so lucky to have. But I wasn't given that choice. My choice was to either follow and believe, or not. I understood the risk, there were never any guarantees. The truth is that we can never escape that risk, be it in a lonely dorm room or across an ocean in the midst of a civil war, whether it be for something great and noble or for nothing at all; with each breath we roll the dice and hope for the best.

There are things in this life that are far worse than death. A grave awaits each of us, and in the grand scheme of things, is being alive for eighty years really any longer than eighteen years? Our life is just a breath, whether we die old and gray or young and vibrant. When death comes for us, it will not matter how many years we managed to preserve our existence but rather what we did with the short time we were given on this earth.

The most horrible and terrifying thing that I can imagine isn't that I would put all that I am on the line for a cause I believe in and then be called on it. The most horrible and terrifying thing is the thought that I could spend my whole existence minimizing the risks I take, living ignorantly convinced of my safety, rejecting the purpose I was created for, and then someday wake up an old man and see that my life has passed before me, and now with death knocking on my door realize that in all my years I have never truly lived.

We each have a destiny, a legend that only we can live. To embrace it is scary and dangerous, and most choose not to. Most put it off until tomorrow, until after high school, until after college, until after establishing a financial base. Can't they see? We only get one shot at this life. Tomorrow may never come. The time is now! Not to drop everything and move to Africa, but to find the passion that is inside us and embrace it, to listen to its subtle whispers.

I do not for one second regret the decision I made to go to Africa. I do not regret the contribution that I made together with my brother. I do not regret sharing a love so deep with my brother that few, even of those blessed with a whole lifetime to spend with their families, will ever know. I do not regret boldly taking hold of every opportunity to live and to love. I do not regret having been able to watch and to help my little brother grow from a boy fresh out of high school into a fearless warrior whose compassion and love were never exhausted despite some of the harshest circumstances in all of creation. I do not regret choosing to stand for good and fight for justice even at the cost of all that was so precious to me. Together Alex and I shared a lifetime's worth of laughs and tears and more wild adventures than most who go to their grave old and gray can claim. My brother, though his life ended senselessly and abruptly, was not shortchanged and I know that he wouldn't have changed a thing about his last year with us.

If I died today, what would my life be for? If today I stood before my maker, what would I have to say about all that I had been given? Alex has stood before God and when asked what he did with what he had been given, my brother could say, "I did all that I could with every single day you gave me."

Will I be able to say the same?

So now I stand at yet another crossroad. The voice inside is whispering again, as if it has any right at all to do so, as if it hasn't already taken enough from me. It says:

Fight; don't give up. Keep going. There is more that I have for you. Someday it will all be made right. Trust.

But I am not as naïve as I once was. I'm not so easily convinced this time. I know the price of following my heart.

But still I'll listen.

Epilogue: Two Years Later

Left to right: Mike, me, and Kris.

Mike reenlisted with the active reserves and is currently training to become a flight medic. He has already told his commanding officers that as soon as he graduates he wants to deploy to Iraq. Within the year he will be air evacking our wounded soldiers out of harm's way to the same hospital that saved Erik's life.

Kris returned to Africa as a volunteer for a Christian adventure tourism company. He is currently in Morocco helping to lead teams through the Sahara Desert on dirt bikes. He will graduate college this spring. He hopes someday to open an adventure ranch to help troubled youth.

Erik made a miraculous, complete physical recovery and returned to the Air Force Academy one year after the bombing. He is still a competitive pole-vaulter at the NCAA Division I level. He is studying political science with an emphasis in international relations.

These three men remain the very best of friends; brothers, bound by blood.

ACKNOWLEDGMENTS

To my mom and dad—thank you for letting us live.

To Mike and Kris, the very best friends a man could ever hope for—thank you, my brothers.

To my family—thank you.

To little Jake, so someday you can know your big brother; he loved you so.

To Will, larry, and General Bagby—thanks for getting me that plane.

To Keith, Rob, John, and Rosa—thank you.

To the Mars Hill community—thank you.

To all of you whose prayers kept me alive—I sincerely thank you.

In loving memory of my brother, Alex
April 22, 1986–April 7, 2005

Until we meet again

We want to hear from you. Please send your comments about this book to us in care of zreview@zondervan.com. Thank you.

ZONDERVAN.com/
AUTHORTRACKER
follow your favorite authors